D0540619

"To Gwen
Happy Christmas "Laughter".
1984.
from Aunt Doris

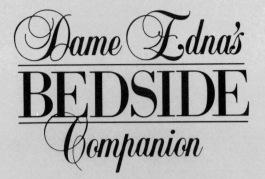

Dame Edna's
BEDSIDE
Companion

Walking the Wombat at Windsor

Dame Edna's BEDSIDE Companion

Crafted by

DAME EDNA EVERAGE

With Forewords by
BEVERLEY NICHOLS
MARGARET DRABBLE
AND BERYL BAINBRIDGE

WEIDENFELD AND NICOLSON LONDON

For my biographer, Julian Jebb,
whose bedside manners are impeccable.

Copyright © Barry Humphries 1982
First published in Great Britain in 1982 by
George Weidenfeld & Nicolson Limited
91 Clapham High Street, London SW4 7TA

All rights reserved. No part of this publication may be
reproduced, stored in a retrieval system, or
transmitted, in any form or by any means, electronic,
mechanical, photocopying, recording or otherwise,
without the prior permission of the copyright holder

ISBN 0 297 78192 8

Design and art direction by Andrew Kay
Illustrations by Daniel Rainey

Printed in Great Britain by
Butler & Tanner Ltd, Frome and London

While this book was in the crafting, Dame Edna's companion, Mrs Douglas
Allsop, underwent some radical naso-labial corrective therapy and
appears in most of the photographs wearing prescribed dressings.
We apologize for any inconvenience this might cause.

NOTE: THIS BOOK CONTAINS NO WHALE PRODUCTS.

CONTENTS AT TIME OF PUBLICATION

DAME EDNA'S PREFACE

World famous astrologers have proved that when it's nighttime in Great Britain it's daytime in Australia and vice versa. Being an old jet setter from way back I can certainly verify this. While we Aussies are at work England sleeps. But spookily enough, while Australia sleeps a surprisingly large percentage of English Possums are still bye-byes as well.

Chances are the computers have already explained this little puzzle in terms of black holes and cosmic rays and I'm certainly not going to blind my Precious Readers with science as they sit propped up in bed nodding off over my Nobel nominated narrative. Suffice it to say that the broad old bosom of Mother England is one of the best places in the world I know for a good old-fashioned snooze – and don't the locals know it!

Chances are British Courtesy and Good Manners are about the first things that hit the drowsy visitor as he lobs into London. In his modest £200-a-night-single-with-bath he can catch up on his jet lag without being woken at the crack of dawn by rush hour traffic. As a unique courtesy to tourists the entire population of the British Isles deliberately goes to work later than any other in the world so as not to disturb pooped panhemispheric pilgrims.

If there's one thing I'm heavily into it's beds and if it wasn't for the time I spend snuggling up with a good book or a bridesmaid I doubt if I'd be the laid-back, unlined miracle of middle-aged motherhood that I am today.

Speaking as a woman who sleeps around in some of the most luxurious hotels and VIP suites on the planet, I know what it's like to wake up wondering where you are and what the dickens you're doing there. It's at moments like these we all need to know where we can reach out and put our finger on a bit of quick consolation – hence this sumptuous volume. I'm not saying it's going to replace the gorgeous Bible that the Gideons have sprinkled in bedside drawers around the globe, but let's face it, Possums, it *could*.

I thought of calling my book *The Gideon Edna*, but decided this was a bit on the uncalled-for side and I'm afraid Good Taste is still my watchword – I'm sorry but it is.

If you study other people's feelings, Dame Nature has a spooky old way of rewarding you a squillion-fold, and frankly it wouldn't surprise me if the Gideon Organization 'came to the party' over a distribution deal on the very book you've got your nose into at the moment. I might even find myself bound into the back of the Good Book if I ever get canon-ized; I'm not saying I will, but more than one person has called me a bit of a Saint, and what a foolish woman I'd be to contradict them.

This book has been handcrafted by the latest British technology to fit comfortably into the decor of contemporary slumber-rooms. Its glossy jacket is resistant (up to a point) to most popular bedside stains such as Ovaltine, Nivea Cream, Johnsons Baby Oil, bickie crumbs and Septojel (Aus. patent pending). After a busy night you can buff up my *Bedside Companion* with a damp chamois or bedside towel. I won't go so far as to say this book is *luminous*, but every effort has been made by the publishers to enable you to see it and reach for it in the dark. That these efforts have failed is no discredit to them.

I hope you're as snug as a bug in a rug as you dip into the second best thing that's ever happened to a woman in bed – let's face it, Possums, what could beat the old hot water bottle!

Dame Edna x

PROLEGOMENA BY BEVERLEY NICHOLS

I happen to be rather a connoisseur of Australian Dames. The greatest of them all, Dame Nellie Melba, was the star of my play *Evensong*, which caused something of a furore in the thirties. Could there be anything in common between Dame Edna and Dame Melba? I hate to admit that there is. Both of them are larger than life, very much larger. A single quotation from Melba, once made in Melbourne to myself when I was in my early twenties, may serve as an illustration. 'I put Australia on the map', she proclaimed. She said it not once but a hundred times and, although she spoke with the tongue of angels, there was an arrogant timbre in the immortal voice that warned against even the thought of contradiction.

The same note was to be heard when she addressed her chauffeur as he drove her to the opera. 'Do not forget', she reminded him, 'that you have a very precious burden in this car.' Dame Edna would have approved of that.

The rakes of the Regency had a charming phrase which fluttered through their conversation when one of their members had behaved in a manner too bizarre for their standards. 'This', they would say, 'is the outside of enough.' Would Edna have incurred their censure? Maybe. Her energy at times is breathtaking, time and again she teeters on the edge of impropriety, but always she redeems by a lightning flash of humour. And in the end one is left with a feeling that there might be a grain of truth in her own verdict on this outrageous volume. I quote: 'A work of deep moral significance, shedding a penetrating light on the problem of our tortured age.'

PROEM BY MARGARET DRABBLE

As an intermittent insomniac who tends to wake at four in the morning shaking with mindless apprehension, I view the prospect of *Dame Edna's Bedside Companion* with something like terror. She frightens the life out of me anyway, and the last thing I thought she could ever be was soporific. After her show at the Theatre Royal Drury Lane, I suffered a prolonged nightmare in which I dreamed I had to appear on stage with her and deliver a two-hour monologue about *au pair* girls. I don't want any more of that kind of thing. But who knows, maybe a whole new way of night life will open up and I will be constantly dipping into this book for 4 a.m. snacks or facial gymnastics. If only her interpretation of dreams included advice on how to keep her out of them.

FOREWORD BY BERYL BAINBRIDGE

I've been an admirer of Edna's for many years and so naturally I welcome her latest work.

With her frank, unashamed love of the minor aspects of life – the home, children, flowers – she has proved an inspiration to her sex.

What an example she is to those more strident members of the Liberation Movement whose message is all up-front and whose womanhood is all behind.

In these worrying days of equality and the triple orgasm, it is refreshing to turn to Edna because we can all identify with her and learn from her.

Hers was not an easy road to hoe and it is typical of the gracious lady she has now become that though she has mentioned, laughingly, in passing, how she was repeatedly forced as a child to pretend to be a wireless, she has not over-emphasized the very real strain it has put upon her.

Mine is not a sycophantic admiration – the hint of acidity in her comments is surely a reflection of those unhappy years – and yet the sadness of her life (Norm's tragic disability, the jealousy of Madge Allsop, those knobs behind the curtain) have not diminished her. That is her strength and her genius. But when, oh when, will she deal seriously with Herpes and the Resurrection?

VESPERS

Megastar kneels at the foot of the bed,
Droops on the Santos watch wistaria head.
Hush! Hush! Whisper who dares!
Dame Edna Everage is saying her prayers.

God bless Madge. I'm feeling woozie.
Wasn't it fun in the new jacuzzi?
Romping around in the bubbling water.
Oh *God bless Valmai* – my problem daughter.

The nightie I'm kneeling in looks rather naff,
But Kenny my son's huddled over his Pfaff,
Running me up some spunky numbers.
God bless Kenny while he slumbers.

Although he's artistic he's a red-blooded male,
And so is his flat-mate, Clifford Smail.
They've hit it off so well together,
Since Cliff won his title: Mr Leather.*

Oh! *Thank you, Dame Nature, for all you've done*
For Brucie, my middle-management son.
And thanks for the gladdy which sprouts from the corm,
And I nearly forgot to say '*God bless Norm*'.

Megastar kneels at the foot of the bed,
Prays for the creature she long ago wed.
If you would interrupt her, then kindly refrain,
Dame Edna is thinking of others again.

*Sydney 1978

This intimate and exclusive pickie needs no explanation, it's just an old Megastar going down on her knees to her Maker.

EDNA'S PLEA

Assume kneeling mode.

Lord:
As I face the daily storm
Let me not forget my Norm
Spoilt and wrapped up nice and warm
Prostrate in his hozzie dorm
Quiescent, like a gladdy corm.
But, if your wonders you perform –
Restoring Norm to ship-shape form –
Pray first, Thy Servant, You inform
(for Heaven's sake).

You may stand.

EDNA'S PRAYER FOR OUR TIME

Lock yourself into ongoing kneeling situation.

Hear my prayer Oh Heavenly Lord
Make me viable across the board
May my bottom line be virtue
Lest I ever bug or hurt You
And help me to unite the nations
In ongoing worship situations.
Uptight and hassled though I be
Help me to be upfront with Thee
And though my input be minute
When Thou my shortfall dost compute
Pray let my daily print-out say
Thy servant was *relevant* per se.

THE MADGNIFICAT

Before I take my forty winks
Pray forgive this wicked minx
Of her conceit I've had a plateful
Just help her to be *faintly* grateful.
Perhaps I've given her too much
And now she treats me like a crutch
Sometimes I fear I'll bend and snap
As selfish Madge tugs on my pap
Of niceness, warmth and generosity
Pray help me to love this old monstrosity.
She came to me without a cent
And all she owns I gladly lent
I've pumped, let's face it, telephone numbers
Into her bank. And now she slumbers.
She who was once so lithe and young
Spare her the rough edge of my tongue.
I should be comforted perhaps
That dear old Madge is under wraps.

THE DESEDNARATA

This magnificent, touching and downright forthright composition, which has been sweetly – and let's face it appropriately – named
after Yours Truly, was found under a dickens of a lot of old wallpaper on a
wall of the Everage homestead in the Australian bush.

No-one has a clue whose old felt-tip laboured away to inscribe
this moving, seminal and slightly over-the-top offering, but the professors
and literary high-flyers amongst us have all gone out on a limb to posit that
it could only have been written by one of my anonymous ancestors, albeit
on Norm's side of the family. I must apologize for an uncalled-for moment
at the end of this otherwise tasteful old pioneer prayer, but our forefathers
on my husband's side of the family were a teeny bit rough and ready and
this last expression about 'biting' is still used in remote parts of the outback
and just means 'pull yourselves together'.

The *Desednarata*, printed on a hand-crafted scroll, is now
hanging in most Australian homes.

GO PLACIDLY, POSSUMS, INTO THE RAT RACE. HEARKEN TO OTHERS, EVEN THE MUTE FOR THEY TOO have a tale to tell. Avoid ratbags, for they are legion and, verily, a pain in the neck. Get your act together and keep interested in your own work ethic for the world is full of cowboys, moonlighters and rip-off merchants. Be yourself. Do not put on the dog or come the raw prawn with your fellow man or woman, even in interpersonal relations. What you miss out on the swings, you'll lose on the roundabouts. Happiness is like a boomerang, so don't chuck it away if you can hold onto it. And if you wear life lightly, like a loose fitting brunch-coat, you have the whole day to look forward to. Like the quokka or the numbat, take every day as it comes. Does the funnel-web spider as she spins look over her shoulder? Come off it. Pull yourself together. Snap out of it. Bite your bum.

THE ARTS OF DROPPING OFF

When you are as busy as I am in the game of Caring and Sharing you never have much trouble going bye-byes. But I tend to suspect that even my workaholic readers don't drive themselves as hard as I do in the funny old business of Loving Thy Neighbour. Don't think I'm boasting, darlings, or 'skiting' (to use an Australian ethnic word), because I'm not. I was given a marvellous gift when I was a bubba and when Dame Nature gave me this precious gift Her only condition was that I shared it with as many people as possible. Hence this beautiful book, which I'm not even writing for the money.

DAME EDNA EVERAGE IS ONE OF THE RICHEST WOMEN IN THE WORLD AND NEED NEVER WORK AGAIN. MOST OF THE PROCEEDS OF HER SHOWS AND PUBLICATIONS GO TO THE ROYAL AUSTRALIAN PROSTATE FOUNDATION. Herr Helmut Honegger, Fellow of the Society of Accountants, Zurich and Lausanne.

But I have not always been a good sleeper. There were times when I lay there waiting for the dawn and I would have given anything for forty winks. The endless nights when my mind churned over and over with the problems of Mankind. I used to worry myself sick about the world's indifference to Australian culture long before I played the decisive role I did in bringing our beautiful poems, operas and recipes to the attention of upmarket connoisseurs. Now, somehow, I'm more relaxed, more 'laid-back' as our Canadian cousins would say.

In Scandinavia there are special clinics for insomniacs and the poor darlings wander round the corridors all night, sometimes for years. It's awful to think there are such troubled folk in a land which produced such gorgeous pictures as Munch's *Scream*.

Here are just a few of *my* insomnia remedies and you don't have to go to Lapland either!

THE LEPROSY METHOD

Chat to each part of your anatomy in turn and tell it to go to sleep. Begin with your toes, then the soles of your feet, then your ankles and so on moving up your body. Take your time and don't move on to a fresh limb until the last one has dropped off.

AUSTRALIAN BOOKS

Another aid which has always worked with me if I'm over-tired and over-excited is reading some wonderful new publication by one of Australia's internationally acclaimed, award-winning, Arts Council subsidized, unknown authors.

COUNTING SHEEP

This traditional method of fighting insomnia comes easily in my wonderful homeland of Australia, and come to that, New Zealand.* Rare indeed is a bedroom window from which the odd baa-lamb cannot be glimpsed. Counting marsupials makes a nice change, though it's sometimes difficult, even in your imagination, getting a posse of Western Australian numbats over a five-bar gate in a hurry.

* New Zealand, as a professor once said, is a country of thirty million sheep – three million of whom think they're human beings!

HERBAL PILLOW

The herbal or hop pillow is an old remedy and I save snagged and laddered panty hose, which I stuff with aromatic Australian shrubs and herbs such as Patterson's Curse, Swagman's Nuisance and Abbo Wort. Gladdy petals also make a very good slumber gusset. Just save the petals, stuff the tights and sleep with a pair of fragrant legs around your neck.

HOT BANANA AND SWEETCORN SMOOTHIE

A soothing nightcap, but for heaven's sake always sit well up in bed to sip your slumber smoothie (see recipe). It's not much use having a good night's sleep if you don't wake up in the morning!

INGREDIENTS

$\frac{1}{2}$ pint hot milk
1 banana
1 small tin sweetcorn

1 tbsp wheatgerm
1 tbsp lecithin or niacin (opt.)
1 jigger of molasses

METHOD

Add ½ hot milk to ingredients. Froth in blender. Pour into long beaker. Top with rest of boiling milk. Garnish with a sprinkle of nutmeg and serve with a couple of boudoir fingers. See pickie page 124.

YIELD: ONE TOOTHSOME SMOOTHIE

MATINÉE JACKET MUNCHING

My marvellous mother told me that when I was a baby I was always jumping up and down in my cot, chatting and singing. She said that this was the first time she ever guessed I was going to be a Megastar, although that word hadn't been invented then. The only way she could get me to snuggle down and drop off was to pop into the cot one of her old matinée jackets for me to suck till the Sandman came. Modern shrinks and know-alls would probably say that this intimate piece of my mother's apparel reminded me of her comforting chest-buttons. What trendy twaddle! As though my darling's boozies could ever be compared with a crushed-mulberry, three ply, lace-ladder-rib-stitched angora cardigan. Come off it!

The night we bundled my marvellous mother off to Melbourne's maximum security Twilight Home, where she has since become a bit of an 'identity', Kenny was helping me stoke the incinerator in the grounds of Everage Hall with some of Mummy's more moth-prone bygones. As the flames licked around her famous collection of hand-knitted matinée jackets, my memories licked around them too. I could even recognize an old rusk-stained, misty pink, laburnum-stitched jacket that my busy bubba-gums had gnawed at many moons ago. Spookily enough, I never gave this much thought until I woke up suddenly one night a few weeks ago on the wrong side of the bed. Fortunately Madge Allsop is a heavy sleeper or she might have put two and two together and made five to find her absent-minded old benefactor sleepily sucking away at her cyclamen seersucker mu-mu. I hasten to add, Readers, that you'd have to be pretty far gone to confuse Madge Allsop's frumpy range of slumber-wear with my mother's scrummy, fully fashioned, frothy bed-boleros.

> By the ruddy light of my mother's combusting bygones I made what Lord Nicolson describes as 'a major literary discovery per se'. Tucked in one of Mummy's gorgeously crafted knitted nooks, I found a smouldering old book in which she had jotted the musings of a lifetime. Thank goodness it didn't go into the incinerator with the rest of my darling's detritus and maternal moth-fodder. See pickie page 34.

FOLLICLE FUMBLING

Did you know there are 100,000 hairs on the scalp? Discover how you compare with the average by counting the number on your head using your thumb and forefinger. Start at the crown and work outwards. When you lose count begin all over again.

FAN YOURSELF OFF

Lie on your back and hold the top of the bedclothes gently with both hands. Lift and drop the bedclothes ten times, but make sure each time you drop them to let go.
WATCH POINT: This method is not advisable if you happen to be in bed with Madge Allsop when she's on one of her hard-boiled egg diets.

THE MARSUPIAL'S MOGADON

Did you know that one of my very favourite marsupials, the Australian Possum, holds the world sleeping record? Possies snooze an average of nineteen hours a day, though I'm afraid it's not just because they're tired. Breathalyze most possums and you'll get a pretty scarey eucalyptus count since, I'm sorry to say, possums are gum-sap junkies who can't even have forty winks without reaching for a fix of foliage. Even our beloved koalas are similarly hooked on uncut leaf. Chances are eucalyptus oil is Dame Nature's natural sedative and *in moderation* it can help us grown-ups in the dropping-off process. That doesn't mean shinning up your nearest eucalypt every night for a gobble of gum tips – a couple of drops of oil on a teaspoon of sugar taken at bedtime should do the trick and it's good for the sniffles as well.

SARAH BERNHARDT'S SEDATIVE

Sarah Bernhardt was my opposite number in the olden days, though I'm afraid we would all have a rude shock if we saw the poor old soul today since she was no oil painting and her Australian popularity was nil to rock-bottom. Nonetheless, in spite of the fact that she had only one leg, she made the most of what was left of her and after a show she always hopped (and I mean that literally) into this soothing and sedative tub.

SARAH BERNHARDT'S BATH

Dame Bernhardt always said the secret of her 'perpetual youth' was an *eau sedative*, which she was bathed with when very fatigued. After being sponged, she dried with a very soft towel and felt so refreshed that she was able to fall asleep at once, even after the most exacting of performances.

INGREDIENTS

2 oz spirits of camphor
1½ cups of sea salt
2 cups alcohol

METHOD

Put all the ingredients in a quart bottle and fill with boiling water. Shake well before using. Add to bath. It leaves the skin smooth and soft and the flesh firm. It is also a defence against wrinkles.

YIELD: ONE REFRESHED ONE-LEGGED ACTRESS

Wise Old Australian Bed Saws

If a lovely snooze you seek
Drink of the phlegm
From a platypus' beak.

Your slumber will be more serene
If you suck the juice
Of a bandicoot's spleen.

You won't need Horlicks
Or a hottie
If you eat the fluff
From a wombat's bottie.

He who holds an emu's fleam
Will sleep all night
Perchance to dream.

You'll snuggle deep in Morpheus' arms
If spawn of jumbuck sprays your 'jarms.

Off like a top you're sure to spin
After half a page
Of Anaïs Nin.

MELTING AWAY
TO MUSIC

A MEGASTAR'S

THINGS THAT MEAN A LOT TO ME

A mantra is a Third World expression for something you mutter over and over again to yourself to get to sleep. Most of the colourful old mantra-mutterers I've noticed bumming around in Bali or the Bahamas, Mustique and Mysore, are more than likely talking a lot of stupid rubbish in the hope that they will bore themselves sufficiently to guarantee a nice snooze-cum-Siesta, when, poor lambs, they generally plonk themselves down in the gutter.

My midnight murmurings are rather more upmarket – I'm sorry but they are, and I never talk to myself anyway. Let's face it, I just have to open my mouth and a couple of thousand paying customers would KILL to 'catch my act' (to use a show business expression). Only when I'm safely alone in bed with my bandaged bridesmaid do these old lips start working, and the result is my very own alphabet – a simple little list of things that mean a lot to this old Megastar.

is for Australia
The land I adore
It's so spotless and clean
You can eat off the floor

is for Boomerang
Which our quaint Abbos launch
In the hope it will bring back
A roast quokka's haunch

is for Culture
Which blossoms unchecked
You can't move in my homeland
For Beckett and Brecht

is for Dingo
Our indigenous pup
You just have to look at him
And he'll gobble you up

is for Explorer
A brave little chap
Who helped put my wonderful land
On the map

MANTRAS

F is for Funnel-Web*
Our furry-legged foe
He sleeps in your slipper
And breakfasts on toe

is for Gladdy, Ginseng, Galle glass
It's also for Glyndebourne where you eat off the grass.
G stands for Gucci, James Galway, Gay Lib
Gallipoli, Galliano, and the four brothers Gibb.
The Golden Goanna is our top film award
And with Genet and Gunter Grass I'm never bored.
Glenda Jackson and Greta Garbo are Gs without peer
So are Gough Whitlam, Gary Glitter and our own Germaine Greer.
To hear Grace Jones sing I'd pay quite a lot for
And Gaddafi's a socialist I've got a soft spot for.
G stands for Graffiti a word that I veto
Since Mature Students have taught me to call it Graffito.
By the end of this poem I'm sure you'll agree
That G is a very special·letter to me

 is for Harrods
My favourite boutique
If you shop there they'll treat you
Like a little-known sheik

 is for invalid
Who'll never come home
I've just given Norm's drip
A new coat of chrome

* Funnel-web (*Agelena consociata*)

25

is for Joylene
My daughter-in-law
In a jumpsuit she skates
On a black rubber floor

is for Kelly
Our radical Ned
When none other dared
He wore a tin on his head

is for Leather
In sling-backs and mules
You should see the accessories
My son's flatmate tools

is for Mould-breaking
What I do best
With the mould on Madge Allsop
I'm put to the test

is for Nivea
Where my digit oft dives
Try it in a sandwich
With finely chopped chives

is for Opera House
An Australian invention
Ideal for Casino
or Business Convention

is for Pizazz
Which makes Paupers happy
They adore my charisma
And I'm raunchy and zappy!

is for Queen
Whom I know very well
She's confided some scorchers
Which I doubt if I'll tell

is for Refinement
Which Australians exude
Don't let some of our Statesmen
Persuade you we're crude

is for Subsidies
The Arts Council keeps giving
Thus sparing our authors
From writing books for a living

is for Thrush
The name of a bird
It's also a yukky old fungus
I've heard

is for Urine
Say 'yuk' if you might
Little jobs keep
Mother's hands soft and white

is for Valmai
My sensitive daughter
She was uptight in Safeways
When security caught her

is for woodwork
At which Madge is improving
She keeps me awake
With her tonguing and grooving

is for X-ellence
Though it's not spelt that way
It's my bottom line
At the end of the day

stands for *The Yell*
And I've got a queer hunch
It's the most gorgeous thing
Ever painted by Munch

is for Zero
A mark I bestow
On once-famous women
Like Margaret Trudeau

THE SECRET OF MY UNFATHOMABLE BEAUTY
MASQUE MARINARA À LA MEGASTAR

Have you ever seen a fish with a dry skin? For that matter, have you ever wondered why fish have such beautiful skin, taking into account the fact of course that they spend comparatively long periods of time in cold salty water, which would play havoc with our epidermal envelopes?

A girl friend of mine, from Sydney, found out this fishy old fact quite by accident and *accident* is the word.

One day when she was swimming near one of Sydney's internationally acclaimed, award-winning beaches, she was radically nibbled by a shark – a ten foot woman-eater! Luckily she kneed it in the stomach, where her knee happened to be at the time. She hopped ashore, lucky girl, slightly shaken but with most of her faculties intact. Spookily enough her intimate struggle with Australia's most famous fish left her skin *softer than it had ever been before.*

Our finny friends secrete precious enzymes which overnight sink deep into famished face tissue. After a Fisherman's Facial I tend to suspect the menfolk will fall for you hook, line and sinker on a large scale and you'll have a whale of a time.

PINOCADO MASQUE

If you want to slam all the doors on your gaping pores and you don't have an allergy to particular fruits and veggies, whip up a pore-pampering Pinocado Masque but make sure that the ingredients are ice-cold.

INGREDIENTS

1 avocado
1 tbsp pineapple juice

METHOD
Peel and pit a nice squashy-ripe avocado. Pulp your pear and slowly add the pineapple nectar (fresh or tinned-fresh) till you have a smooth mixture. Pineapple syrup contains an enzyme that attacks skin debris, face-flake and helps close yawning pores. The avocado feeds, oils and vitamizes the skin.

Remove all make-up before applying your Pinocado Masque to all areas of the face and neck. Wear your masque for approximately ten minutes. Remove with cotton wool balls soaked in pineapple juice. Pat dry.

Before the plunge

My beauty-bait

A plaice and a crab
leave your face feeling fab

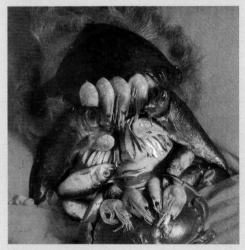

A yawn with a prawn
and a kip with a kipper

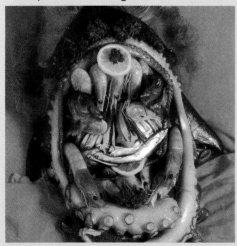

Octopus for glamour-puss

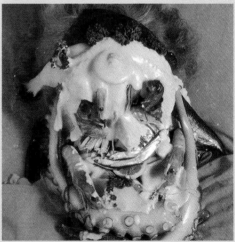

My Thousand Island glamour garnish

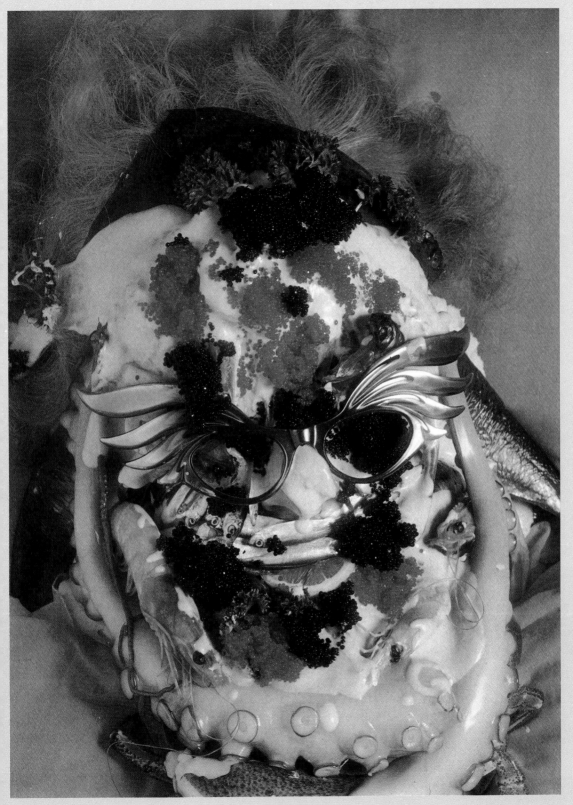

A sturgeon a day
keeps the surgeon (cosmetic) away.

SLEEPY-TIME DAME

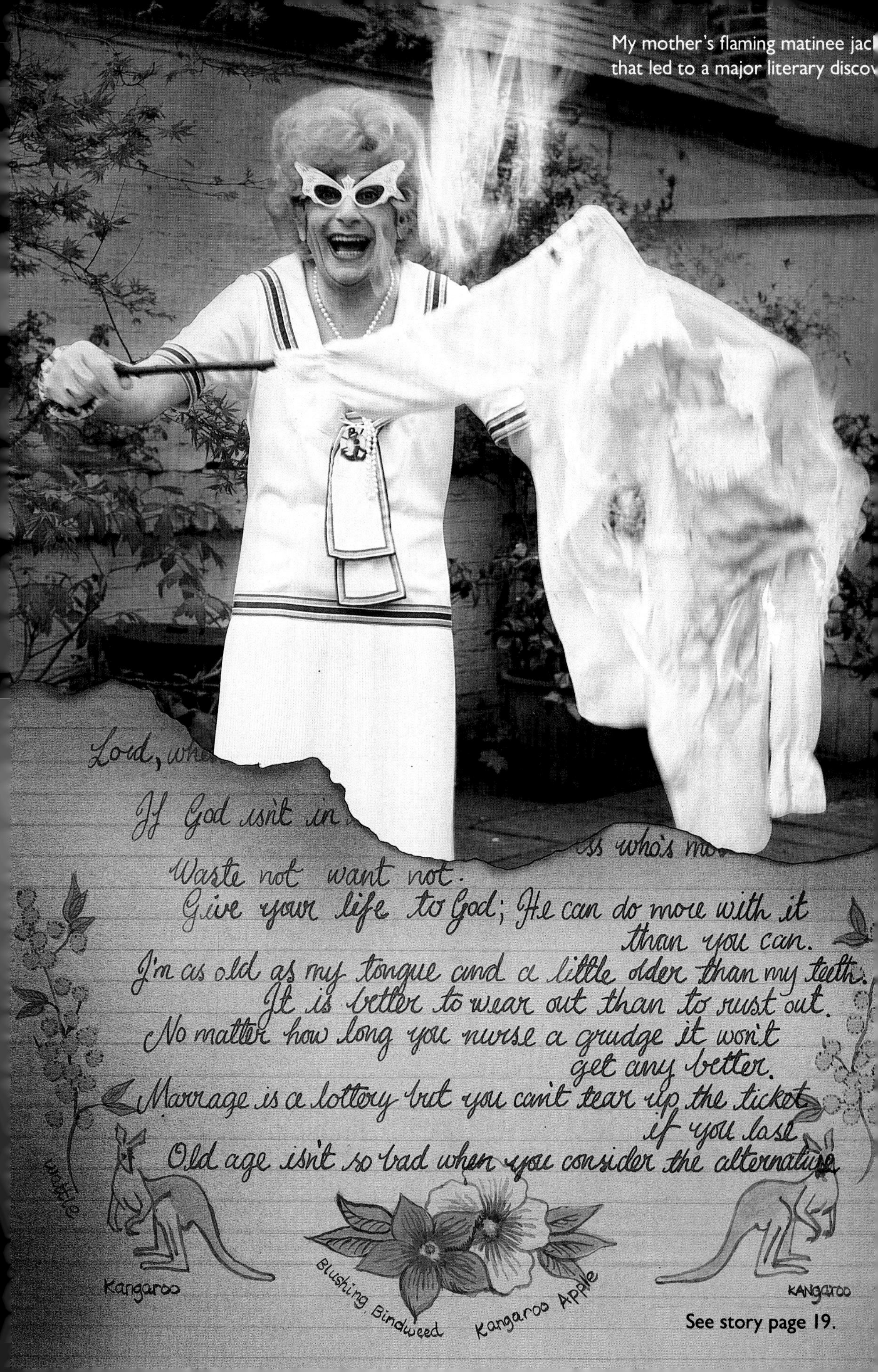

Lord, whe
If God isn't in
ss who's mo
Waste not want not.
Give your life to God; He can do more with it than you can.
I'm as old as my tongue and a little older than my teeth.
It is better to wear out than to rust out.
No matter how long you nurse a grudge it won't get any better.
Marrage is a lottery but you can't tear up the ticket if you lose.
Old age isn't so bad when you consider the alternative.
wattle
Kangaroo
Blushing Bindweed
Kangaroo Apple
KANgaroo

My mother's flaming matinee jac
that led to a major literary discov

See story page 19.

Video Vigil

The Bedside Drawer in History

I tend to suspect that there is no more accurate clue to the human personality than the humble bedside drawer per se. Throughout the ages everyone has had a bedside drawer of some description, and though a Stone Age bedside drawer would strike us today as a bit rough and ready and even infra dig, it possessed a lot of the amenities and appointments we have – if you only scratched the surface. Archaeologists of my acquaintance spend a *lot* of time scratching beneath the surface and, after poking around in caves, nooks and crannies, have found definite traces of bedside drawers on either side of the flat, so-called 'sleeping-stone' employed by our horny-hipped forefathers. Fragments of bone, tipped with mammoth fluff – yes, Stone Age ancestor of the cotton wool bud – have been unearthed in their thousands, proving that prehistoric Man and Woman had their ears very much to the ground in terms of aural hygiene.

Rude stone vessels have also been excavated in antediluvian dormitories, oozing with traces of pteradactyl blubber and perfumed with primeval fungi (Neanderthal Nivea!), which forensic wallahs have determined even now retains the power to make Neanderthal women attractive at the end of the day.

Moving on, the Medieval Middle Ages provide their own treasure trove for the bedside sociologist. An old EEC-type expression *droit de seigneur* meant that the Lord of the Manor – or the Bishop – could at any time, day or night, 'check out' the top drawer of a virgin's vestibule for the odd giveaway geegaw.

But the bedside drawer really came into its own when Marie Antoinette held sway. When heads were rolling all over the EEC every upper-echelon high flyer in Gay Paree, in fact top drawer people in general, kept everything ready for a quick getaway tucked in a secret nook beside their divans, chaise longues and couchettes.

But my own wonderful homeland of Australia (I'm an Australian incidentally Readers) was almost the last country in the world to introduce this type of bedroom facility. Aroused early by kookaburras screaming with laughter in the garden shrubs, our rugged pioneers had no need of alarm clocks or the reading matter and analgesics that are so indispensable to the modern Australian. So the early convicts transported Down Under were bound to be disappointed if they were on the look-out for the odd bedside bonanza or even a mattress they could ransack for someone's lifetime savings.

Our Aboriginals did not see the point of either of these modern appurtenances and they are not mentioned or depicted in early explorers' accounts. I dread to think what an Aboriginal might have in a bedside

Top left Dame Edna's bedside table (a mock-up, for security purposes). *Bottom left* A typical British bedside table. *Top right* A typical Australian bedside table. *Centre right* Mrs Douglas Allsop's bedside table. *Bottom right* My daughter Valmai's bedside receptacle.

drawer if he had one. The mind boggles but I tend to suggest that old bones for pointing at folk, spare boomerangs and anti-uranium literature would probably jostle each other for drawer space in the ethnic bedside table.

I'm a pretty upfront old Megastar from way back so I'm going to confess to you now that whenever I am visiting someone's home, officially or unofficially, I can never resist a peek into their bedside drawers. What normal red-blooded woman can, let's face it? And do me favour, I'm an investigative journalist. On the pretext of slipping off to powder my nose I always manage to cast an expert eye in my hostess's bedroom bureau, and if possible I also make a point, if I can, of checking out hubby's little cubby. I do this not because I'm nosy. Heavens alive I've got more to do than 'sticky-beak' around my neighbours' nooks of nocturnal necessities! But I do it in a *nice* way, Possums. I do it because, quite frankly, my ceaseless intellectual curiosity *forces* me to learn all I can about mankind's most intimate little doings.

A poem I once wrote (this morning) says it all.

Nature is red in tooth and claw
Inside the humble bedside drawer
Midst soiled buds and cotton balls
The genie of the jungle calls
When day is done and darkness lingers
What better place for eager fingers
To fumble frolic and explore
Than deep within a bedside drawer.

My pictures graphically show what I'm driving at. In a way I'm sorry they had to reproduce a snap of my daughter Valmai's tell-tale table, but she'll never get well if I keep on protecting her like I do. I'm sorry but she won't. Madge's bedside table tells its own tragic tale and our hidden cameras have captured a typical Australian bedside bureau in marked contrast to the pitiful little Third World UK variety with its pools coupons and vandalized telephone. The photograph of my own slumber-side amenities is a 'mock-up', Possums. My security advisers said that if my real telephone were to appear in a snap I'd be in danger of being dialled by every deviant's digit in the district.

Why I Can't Sleep Alone

Sleeping With Your Son – A Mother's Anguish

I'll never forget the lonely night my husband Norm was whisked off to the hozzie. 'Is everything all right Mum?' I heard Kenny's hoarse whisper as I sobbed into the pillow.

For the next few weeks of hoping and praying Kenny and I kept a round-the-clock telephone vigil and when the instrument finally rang with the thrilling news that my beloved husband was to be the recipient of the world's first successful prostate transplant, it was my son who cradled me in his jarma'd arms as I wept tears of joy into his warm winceyette.

I think it was Norm himself who suggested that I make contact with my old bridesmaid Madge Allsop, whose husband, Douglas, had left her without a penny. 'A woman like you needs company,' his eyes seemed to say in the misty mirror above his page-turning machine. In offering Madge Allsop my mother's old room at Everage Hall, Moonee Ponds, Melbourne, I had not bargained for a fully-paid-up card-carrying somnambulist in the house.

By this time Kenny was staying away from home for the occasional long weekend discussing business and Barbara Stanwyck with his sympathetic flatmate-to-be, Clifford Smail, and I didn't want to worry him sick by telling him how many times I'd had to coax my disoriented and out-to-it old bridesmaid off the garage roof and back to her bed. I was never quite sure how genuine her little nocturnal strolls really were, and to what extent she wasn't on another of her ego trips. A cry for help isn't always a cry for help. Think that one over for a minute, Possums! Anyway it was a short hop, step and a jump from the garage roof to my own bed where Madge has now taken up her permanent abode.

Will I, who give so much to so many, never know more than a moment's solitude? On a rare night of peace when Madge was off on one of her walkabouts and a wicked gremlin inside me was hoping and praying for a loose tile, I wrote this tender lyric.▶

THE FABRIC OF MY LIFE

There's something about my man I'll ne'er forget:
His winceyette.
Each night when I turned off our TV set
And crept beneath our old mosquito net
Into our double bed I'd gently get
And there asleep I'd spy my darling pet
In winceyette.

Now years have passed
His place there at my flank
Is taken by a form huddled and dank
Who in the daytime treats me like a bank
And when night falls –
To be completely frank –
Deserves a jolly good old-fashioned spank!

I still wake up beside her damp with sweat
And thoughts gnaw at my being and fancies fret
That Norm so far away is with me yet
Swathed in that fabric that I'll ne'er forget
Pure winceyette.

BEDSIDE COMPANIONS

WHO I'D LIKE TO SLEEP WITH AND WHY

Sleeping together, in inverted commas, has taken on a permissive meaning lately that Dame Nature never intended, so when I tell you just a few of the celebrities of yesteryear with whom I would like to share forty winks, don't run away with the idea that playing hospitals is my bottom line at the end of the day.

Leonardo da Vinci, Orson Welles, Johannes Brahms, Rosa Luxemburg, Stalin and Scott Fitzgerald are just a few personalities I'd love to share my sheets with, but, although I've still got all the drives and juices of a healthy red-blooded Australian woman at the height of her powers, I would no more want to 'play hospitals', as you call it, with say Rosa Luxemburg than fly to the moon. Anyway, I'm pretty certain that this wonderful old social worker is no longer in the Land of the Living and I'd be a pretty unwell type of a woman – in fact a moral write-off – if I tried to commit intimacy with a skeleton of my own sex! Let's face it, you wouldn't be reading this sumptuous publication if I was a ghastly type of deviant from Down Under, would you?

'So why Dama Edna?' I can hear you cry. 'Why hop into the cot with these famous laypersons?'

Let me explain. Have you ever woken up to find your sleeping partner has been thinking along the same lines as yourself? What woman hasn't? This is scientific proof that when we sleep we more often than not share little thought waves with our hubbies. In my book, *The Symbiosis of Slumber: Critique and Context*, I'm going to go into all this in a lot more scientific detail, but for the purposes of my *Bedside Companion*, which is being perused by a broad-based, grass-roots readership of non-technical, and in many cases foolish and stupid people, I'll keep it simple. People who snooze together, fuse together.

Chances are, I tend to suspect, that if old Leonardo da Vinci's hairy top-knot was on the pillow next to yours tonight you'd wake up next morning with a silly smile on your chops like his clever cartoon of the Mona Lisa. I'll spare you, as I said, all the scientific ins and outs but a little lie-in with Leonardo could have you grinning your lips off all day long and inventing aeroplanes and pop-up toasters non-stop, just like that tufty old Tuscan technician. Spooky, but true.

I was a pioneer of the internationally acclaimed and award-winning Australian film industry, so cuddly old cineaste, Orson Welles, would be soaking up quite a few of my brain waves if we ever shared a blanket. *Citizen Kane* is one my favourite videos, incidentally, along with *Apocalypse Now* and *Mrs Miniver*, and Orson and I are old buddies from way back. When our letters are published (*Orson and Edna, The Orson*

Leonardo da Vinci   Orson Welles   Johannes Brahms

Rosa Luxemburg   Joseph Stalin   F. Scott Fitzgerald

Welles/Dame Edna Everage Correspondence, in five volumes with an introduction by Alexander Walker) the world will learn that I was one of the first
kiddies in Australia to appreciate *Citizen Kane*. I wrote off a little p.c. to
dear old Orson then and we've been pen pals ever since.

Johannes Brahms is probably the best known composer of
lullabies in the world so what better palliasse pal to have crooning his latest
chart-topping lullaby on the next pillow?

My choice of Stalin might surprise European readers who
believe everything they read in the papers, but I'm here to tell you that the
Political Science Departments of Australian Universities have pretty well
proved that Stalin wasn't the scallywag he's made out to be by elitist reds-
under-the-bed Enemies of the People. Far from it. 'Uncle Joe' was, I tend to
suspect, a seminal and pivotal mould-breaking Muscovite.

Scott Fitzgerald is another much-maligned Cinderella of
showbiz. He'd have me laughing all night with his priceless witticisms like
when he said to Anaïs Nin (another of my very special people) 'The rich are
different from you and me, Anaïs.' Goodness me, Possums, it must have been
hard to keep a straight face with old F. Scott around in his Brideshead-style
jim-jams.

Incidentally I wouldn't have minded an hour or two under
Edvard Munch's Danish doona.* I've got a funny feeling he was a real
scream.

* Scandinavian for duvet.

WOMEN IN WOODWORK

Madge Allsop crafting herself a 'high tech' camp bed. I've lost count of the number of times I've said to Madge, 'Go make your bed and lie in it as well, woman.' Little did I know she had some kind of a degree in oxyacetylene welding, which probably explains why her hands are the roughest pair of paws that have ever toyed with my nightie straps. This spooky shot makes old Madge look a bit like a cross between the Mummy's Curse and the Texas Chain Saw Monster trying out a gruesome new gadget.

BIZARRE BYW

I tend to suspect a lot of my readers' eyebrows are going to shoot up when they see the title of this chapter. Over the years I've become a bit of a custodian of world morals and I am well aware that parents will probably be giving this publication to troubled teenage kiddies hoping against hope that some of my womanly wisdom and tasteful advice rubs off. So please be reassured that the sensitive areas I'm now about to fearlessly probe will be probed in the most tasteful way possible.

Chances are the honeymoon night still holds its horrors for most young couples and this is largely because we cannot always be sure what our partner is going to do after he's shaken the confetti out of his shoes and checked out the room service menu a couple of times. I well remember a queer phrase of my wonderful mother's that came back to me on my own honeymoon night: 'Some men don't like it plain and simple', she croaked. I never asked my darling what she meant at the time – kiddies rarely do encourage their parents to elaborate when the subject of hospitals crops up, but I followed Mummy's gaze to the top of her wardrobe where my father always kept a mysterious little black suitcase that we were never allowed to look in. Then I looked back at my mother and for a second I swear there was a hint of horror in her big brown, prematurely open eyes (I'd just woken her up with a cup of tea). I never did see the contents of Daddy's box, but now I'm a Sophisticated International Megastar with chums like Jack Nicholson, Orson Welles, Sylvia Kristel, Roman Polanski and April Ashley, I've been forced to admit that the odd thing goes on behind locked bedroom doors that would make my old Daddy's portmanteau look as innocent as a Masonic apron. Spookily enough my father *was* a Mason incidentally.

Fetishism is a new word to me so chances are, I tend to suspect, you've never heard of it either. Am I being too permissive and upfront when I say that fetishism by and large is some special little thing that 'turns you on'? It's all supposed to start when you are a kiddie, so the medical men say – about the age when we start playing doctors and nurses at school and ask our parents those awkward little questions. Some queer quirk gets caught in a nook of our brains and for ever afterwards we only have to think of it to get a bit romantically inclined.

I once had a terrible crush on Mr Choate, my arithmetic teacher, who was always hitting his blackboard duster with a ruler and giving off enormous puffs of chalk dust. I never thought about it again until I suddenly remembered my first glimpse of Norm, my husband-to-be. He was always a nervous boy and suffered terribly from dandruff, poor Possum. One day in Sunday School I saw him slapping away at the shoulders of his

Sunday best trying to dislodge the clinging clouds of cradle-cap and spookily enough it didn't seem a scrap yukky, in fact my hands got so trembly and damp a bit of hymn book came off on them. Many years later dear old Norm used to wonder why I loved dusting him with talcum at blanket bath time and swishing it off with a ping-pong bat. I wondered myself actually, but now modern science has explained that I am as normal as the next woman.

Mind you, I can't say I'd like to be turned on *all the time*. I'd feel like a tap. Chances are old Dame Nature has invented all these squillions of funny fetishes to add a little spice and seasoning to the average marriage. We are all fetishists, I tend to suspect, not just a few ghastly types prowling around Soho looking at pricey snaps of Danish lasses in PVC suspender belts. These wretches are the unacceptable face of fetishism. And my porn pal Ms Mary Whitehouse sees eye to eye with me on that one.

When you encourage the man in you life to put on a nice tie, instead of those frightful open-necked shirts and gold fob chains I get so tired of in Fulham* and Double Bay,† you are probably reliving some weird little girlhood moment when you strangled one of your dollies. Under these circumstances it's never a good idea to tell him this or romance could fly out of the window and your beau with it. But there's just a chance he could have a similar little kink, for instance, as a kiddie he might have dreamt he was a dolly being strangled, so if his eyes light up on Father's Day when you unveil yet another gorgeous Italian cravat, it's a pretty sure sign you've found a fetish-friend for yourself and this could lead to hours of unbridled passion you never thought possible.

A famous politician I knew met his first sweetheart at a children's party. When he gave her an innocent little peck he noticed to his excitement that she had a crumb of creamy birthday cake clinging to her upper lip. When I learned this I was able to offer his deeply troubled wife a great deal of womanly comfort and wisdom. You see until then the poor creature could never understand why every time her man came home from work he slapped her across the chops with a three-tiered coffee cream gateau. Now she has accepted this harmless little expression of her husband's affection she participates with joy and gratitude instead of skulking in a wardrobe at the sound of his eager footfall and the rustle of his parcel from the local patisserie. Now she flings open the front door wearing an attractive plastic shower cap and a see-through waterproof bib.

Chances are the clever person who wrote the delightful ditty 'All of Me, Why Not Take All of Me' was probably inspired by a fetishist loved one who only liked bits of him at a time. Some folk I'm told, are *into shoes* in a big way and it's spooky to think many of them probably have jobs

* Fulham; a frightful part of London enjoying a temporary vogue.
† Double Bay; a frightful part of Sydney enjoying a temporary vogue.

in the footwear departments of our family department stores, running around back and forth with their arms full of shoe boxes and sliding those chilly little measuring machines under our unsuspecting tootsies. Something probably happened to them at the bootee stage of infancy, when a nice salesperson fitted them for something a bit sturdier and accidentally did something pretty radical to their circulation at the same time.

I ténd to suspect it's the menfolk who succumb to this particular foible. A girlfriend of mine once came home unexpectedly after walking out half-way through a permissive Arts Council Subsidized Show to find her hubby hobbling around the home in her favourite pair of patent leather courts. I'm afraid my friend took it rather badly and if only she'd had a copy of this informative volume sooner they could have been solemates.

Chances are that if couples were a bit franker with each other about their little quirks ghastly misunderstandings like this would never arise. Early in my own married life I confessed a guilty little preference to my inexperienced husband, Norm. In those days Norm (later Lord Everage) was still living at home and although he had already felt a few tell-tale twinges, his slippered feet had still a very long way to shuffle along the road to International Urological Stardom. There seemed to be something wrong with the physical side of our intimate home life, and I was wracking my brains for some simple means of saving our soon-to-be-famous marriage. Suddenly I spied, lying on a formica table top a squelchy pair of rubber gloves – can you guess what's coming Possums? Next to them I saw an old Irish linen apron – with lovely Australian scenes all over it and marsupials and aborigines creeping in and out – which I had adored as a kiddie in the bush. I looked at these limp old garments and I looked at my cross-patch spouse. It came to me in a flash and I'm happy to say it came to him as well. Like a sleepwalker Norm shuffled across the kitchen and slid his digits into the big pink gauntlets while I caringly tied my ethnic apron firmly and lovingly behind his back. As his virile wrists plunged automatically into the washing-up we knew without a word being uttered that we had embarked upon a new, enduring and meaningful phase in our relationship. He never looked more vulnerable or desirable. Until a few years ago when his prostate struck him down and the doctors told him to try to cut down on housework our marriage was the stuff legends are made of. I thanked my lucky stars at the time. Now I know better. Thank you Fetishism.

Dame Edna's Bedside Bookclub

Nod Off with Your Nose in Something.

MICRONOVEL

This internationally acclaimed old novel has been miniaturized for your convenience. If you like popping under the bedclothes with a torch, this is it. My old eyes don't miss much, Possums, but the odd Senior Citizen with a low-carrot diet may have to peer a bit to read this moving masterpiece.
WATCHPOINT: SENIORS, SPECS PLEASE!

REMS

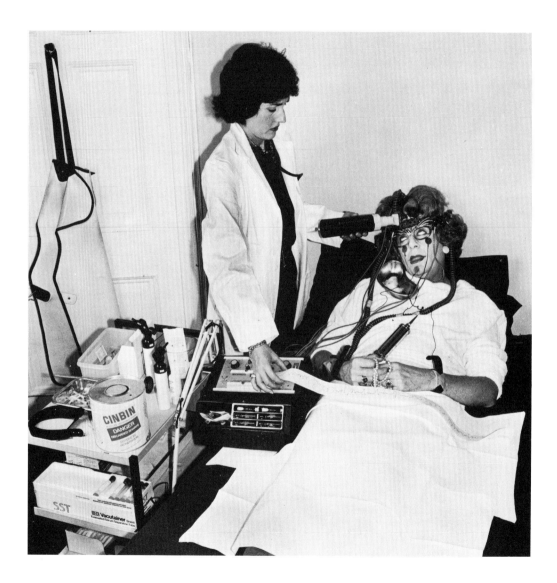

Dr Ida Lichter, an adorable Red Sea Pedestrian from Melbourne, pictured here fumbling with my latest print-out as she measures and calibrates my Rapid Eye Movements or REMS. This gorgeous medico can wire me up *anytime*.

DREAMS

MADGE ALLSOPP'S NIGHTMARE

I suppose I can smile at it now. Well, I could, except for the stitches. And E can just about crack a smile when the subject is raised. Which is *often*, by her.

But at the time I can tell you it was *no laughing matter!* I remember it vividly. I brought E her tea and Press clippings as per usual on that fateful morning. She was propped up on all the pillows, with a knowing look in her unmade-up eyes, when she came out with it. As she spoke I noticed to my surprise and horror that her lovely, almost crepe-free throat was encircled by mysterious mauve markings. Jean Batterby once told me behind the shelter-shed at school that these are called 'Love-Bites'. Those purple blemishes had not been on Edna's neck when we retired, and I hardly thought that it was to these that E wished to refer.

'Madge,' she said rather casually, 'I've just run through last night's video, and I think there's a snatch you'd be interested in.' (E has her every *movement* video-taped for posterity, hence the pickies in this book.) I put down the tray. Edna wiped her hands clean of Nivea and prodded the 'play' button on the monitor. Sure enough, up came the all-too-familiar nocturnal scene – the two of us tucked up like two peas in a pod. Then, to my horror, I was seen to lash out savagely in the darkness of the bedchamber. As Edna froze the frame, so I froze too. There, for all the world to see was the nightmarish moment E has chosen to reproduce here in her new book. 'What the dickens is *that* all about?' snapped E. 'You'll have to come up with a pretty good explanation for this my girl – and I've got a rough idea of what the subject of your essay for *today* is, you minx.' I remember thinking she made that last word sound *negative* and *uncalled for*. I stood expressionless – probably something to do with my new cosmetic facial dressings. 'And you can wipe that silly look off your bandages too,' she chided.

Pen and paper were provided and I struggled to recall what demon could have possessed me at 3.10 a.m. that morning. And then it came to me. It arose from the horrible set-to that E and I had had that evening prior to beddy-byes.

I had long been an admirer of Sir Rolf Harris, the crooner, an admiration equalled in my book only by my devotion to E. But for some reason or other that latter Megastar had, on the evening of my nightmare, chosen to rob me of one of my few pleasures in life (now that my husband, Douglas, has been gathered) – dozing off to the strains of Sir Rolf and his wobbly boards, etc. She had confiscated my Harris collection and played, instead, her Horace Heidt nostalgia 78s.

A firm favourite of mine from Sir Rolf's repertoire has always been that song about the two little boys that used to play with each other,

and as I lay there sobbing I tried to rewrite the song about E and myself –
two little *girls* who were very close to each other. As I dozed off, I saw E and
myself hopping around the Aussie bushland like a couple of young joeys. In
those days I often took the lead as E was a bit of a 'sook'. I was leaping
along this track when suddenly there it was! Like a jack-in-the-box this
yukky pink slithery thing sprang out at me from behind a gum tree. A giant
clammy old snake. Spookily enough – as E would say – this horrible Australian reptile had just *one eye*, which it hungrily fixed on me. I'd never seen
anything like it, nor have I to this day to tell the truth.

Sparing no thought for myself – for I could hear E hopping
gaily along after me and I feared she would be bitten – I grabbed out at the
thing, throttling and squeezing and holding on, till it evaporated in my
hands and crumbled away to nothing.

It was then I woke up. To my horror I found that the yukky
clammy tissue I was throttling was beloved E's neck! And you can imagine
the atmosphere in our bedroom was pretty unpleasant as I lay there trem-
bling, dreading the rough edge of E's tongue. By morning I had 'blacked-
out' the horror of the night.

The upshot of the affair is that E now insists that I wear bells
on all my extremities at nighttime in case I ever get the 'urge', as she puts it,
again. I suppose she has enough stresses and strains in her life without
having to keep an eye on her faithful bridesmaid around the clock in case
she has stupid dreams about one-eyed pink snakes.

A FINCHLEY DOCTOR WRITES:

'This is the dream of a pathetically inadequate woman with a great deal of suppressed aggression and anger. Snake dreams usually occur when the dark instinctual levels of existence are repudiated and rejected by the conscious mind, which is then more threatened than ever by them. The snake is also the archetype of the devil who seduced Eve in the serpent's guise. It can also relate to an inner state of apprehension or to an actual danger that must be overcome. The colour of the snake, in this case pink, could help us pin down the significance of this dream if we knew what the colour pink signified to this patient or, if the dreamer had ever had any disagreeable transactions with monocular, or bigoted persons. The dream encounter takes place in the 'Australian bush', which symbolizes unconsciousness. I fear for this woman. She needs help.'

EDNA'S DREAM

I have this recurring dream that I'm standing on the stage of one of the biggest and most prestigious theatres of the world, in a gorgeous frock, throwing costly long-stemmed flowers into the auditorium and singing a beautiful song composed by myself. The audience, numbering many thousands, has risen to its stamping feet and is clapping and cheering and throwing streamers. I feel a pleasurable sensation quivering through my entire organism and I wake up to find that it is really happening.

ANOTHER FINCHLEY DOCTOR WRITES:

'I have been given no information about the profession of this dreamer, but I would guess from her dream that she is a hyper-intelligent and sensitive person, possibly world famous and associated with the arts. If she has a fault, it is that she cares too little for herself and too much for others. There is much that she could teach the medical profession.'

The Musings of a Megastar

I'm an intensely private person

I'm sorry but I am....

My Swiss advisers tell me I never need to work again

But I have so much to give...so much to share

I'm a survivor

And so is my husband . . . just

Spookily enough I'm grateful for his little prostate problem

It's taught me acceptance

I *could* be the first C of E saint

If I wasn't basically a warm woman with strong drives and juices.

Nodding off to Knowledge

Australians learn more in their sleep than any other nation in the world, computers have proved. Why waste hours of slumber having stupid dreams that you can hardly ever remember when you could be plugged into some of the most advanced educational hardware outside the Smithsonian Institute?

Here's me freshening up on the uxorilocal Abbos of the Murrumbidgee Basin, one of the popular courses offered by the Open University of Sydney.

Frankly it wasn't a subject I was terribly *into* when I dropped off, but by brekky time I was in the Mastermind class in terms of matrilinial kinship per se.

It's advisable in sleeplearning, Possums, to wear stereo headphones. If you pump some of these upmarket Uni courses through your standard stereo speakers you'll be over-educating your neighbours to the point where they could become unbearable, and let's face it, we all live in pretty close proximity to folk for whom a little knowledge goes a long, *long* way! Not only did I become in a few short hours a world authority on the habits of our dusky brothers in the Murrumbidgee Basin, but I actually learnt *more* than I ever wanted to know on this subject. Much, *much* more. Now, between you and me, I just want to forget. Oh that there were a sleeplearning course for that!

Before I was a Megastar or even a Superstar I used to write my own scripts for my wonderful stage shows and Madge Allsop would then mutter them over and over again in my ear as I slept. After a few nights I would wake up word perfect, though Madge usually looked a bit the worse for wear and often had to be popped into a nursing home for a couple of days. I suppose this proves pretty conclusively that I invented sleeplearning. It certainly explains why poor old Madge started thinking she was me, and let's face it, Possums, if you live close to a genius and even repeat their utterances over and over again, your own personality is more than likely to fly out of the window, particularly if, like Madge, you have little or no personality whatsoever to start with.

Laid to rest

MY POSITION ON SLEEP

Marilyn

Moroccan method

Semaphore

Flamenco fandango

The koala curl

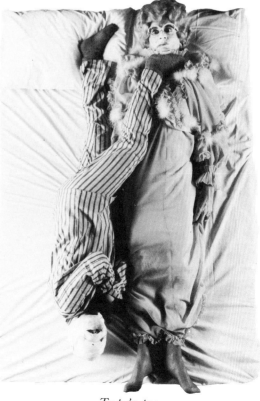

Top 'n toe

Truckling Australian style

The aftermath of a nightmare or wrestling with sleep

Human bolster

Shrinks say Madge Allsop wants to get back to the womb, but why does it always have to be mine?

Midnight Memos

Funny dream — audience <u>not</u> laughing.

Phone Dr. Rosenblatt for <u>interpretation</u>

Telex Sister Younghusband re filling Norm's saline drip with brandy butter for <u>Chrissie.</u>

SAY NO TO <u>VOGUE!</u>

Tell Niarchos next weekend out of the question.

<u>Sell</u> Tasmanium titanium <u>Buy</u> Onyx futures.

Phone Pope!

Authorize thousand dollar donation to Australian Save the Shark Foundation

Demand latest book sales print-out from Lord Nicolson

When you're an ideas woman with a Renaissance mind like mine, chances are you're up and down all night scribbling little notes to yourself to peruse on the morrow. This is just a random page from one of my bedside pads, which I forgot to give to the man from the Humanities Archive Department of the University of South Carolina when he called last week to empty my wastepaper basket.

This page has been generously donated by the publishers for the reader's very own dreams, waking thoughts, random ramblings and automatic writings (for which the publishers cannot be held responsible).

THE FACIAL GYM

MY EPIDERMAL AEROBICS

These never-before-published pickies show me giving my famous face its nightly work-out to music. It's a pity this isn't a talking book or you'd hear the gorgeous strains of Sir Michael Tippett or Horace Heidt in the background as I knead and nourish my nooks and nodules.

The biggest organ . . .

a woman has . . .

63

and, arguably, the most visible . . .

is her skin.

I keep mine Megastar moist . . .

with Dame Nature's ten tools

Let's face it. I'm a woman who uses her head...

and vice versa!

Keep 'in touch' with the biggest organ you've got. Win with skin.

SLEEPING AROUND THE WORLD

THE EVERAGE REPORT

I very much enjoyed my night with the Red Sea Pedestrian though if you are planning a similar experience remember to politely decline should he offer to *lend you anything* during the wee small hours.

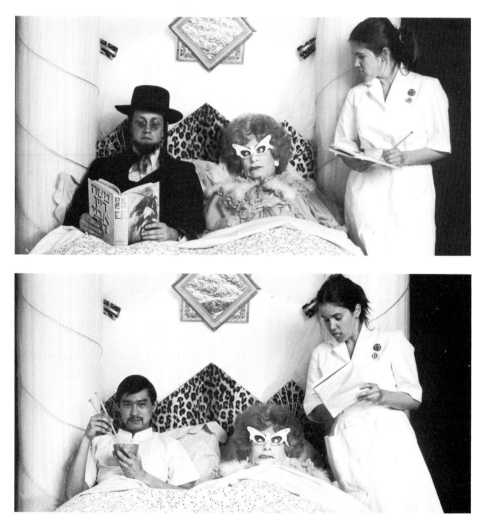

Little Chang Zin Sang is oriental, in case you hadn't taken a long hard look at the accompanying snap. One of the spooky things about going to bed with a Chinaman is that you wake up in the morning still feeling sleepy.

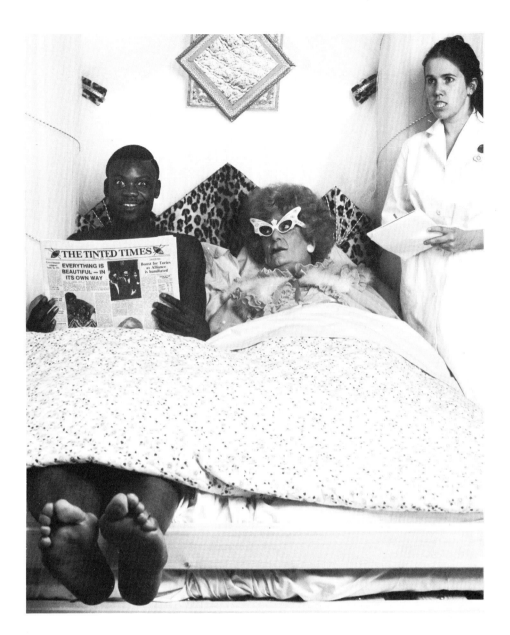

My unprepossessing research assistant, Jane, monitored my night with Patrick, a delightful and statuesque Third World person from a tinted part of the globe. He was one of Nature's Gentlemen though I did insist he kept both hands firmly on his tabloid throughout the night. I can however confirm that he was considerably longer than any man I've ever gone through a form of sleep with.

Rest assured Readers that all these multiracial sleeping experiments were strictly supervised and scientifically computer-monitored. Although you can't see it in our pictures we were trussed up like chickens under the bed clothes and plugged into one of the most sophisticated pieces of hardwear I've ever slept with.

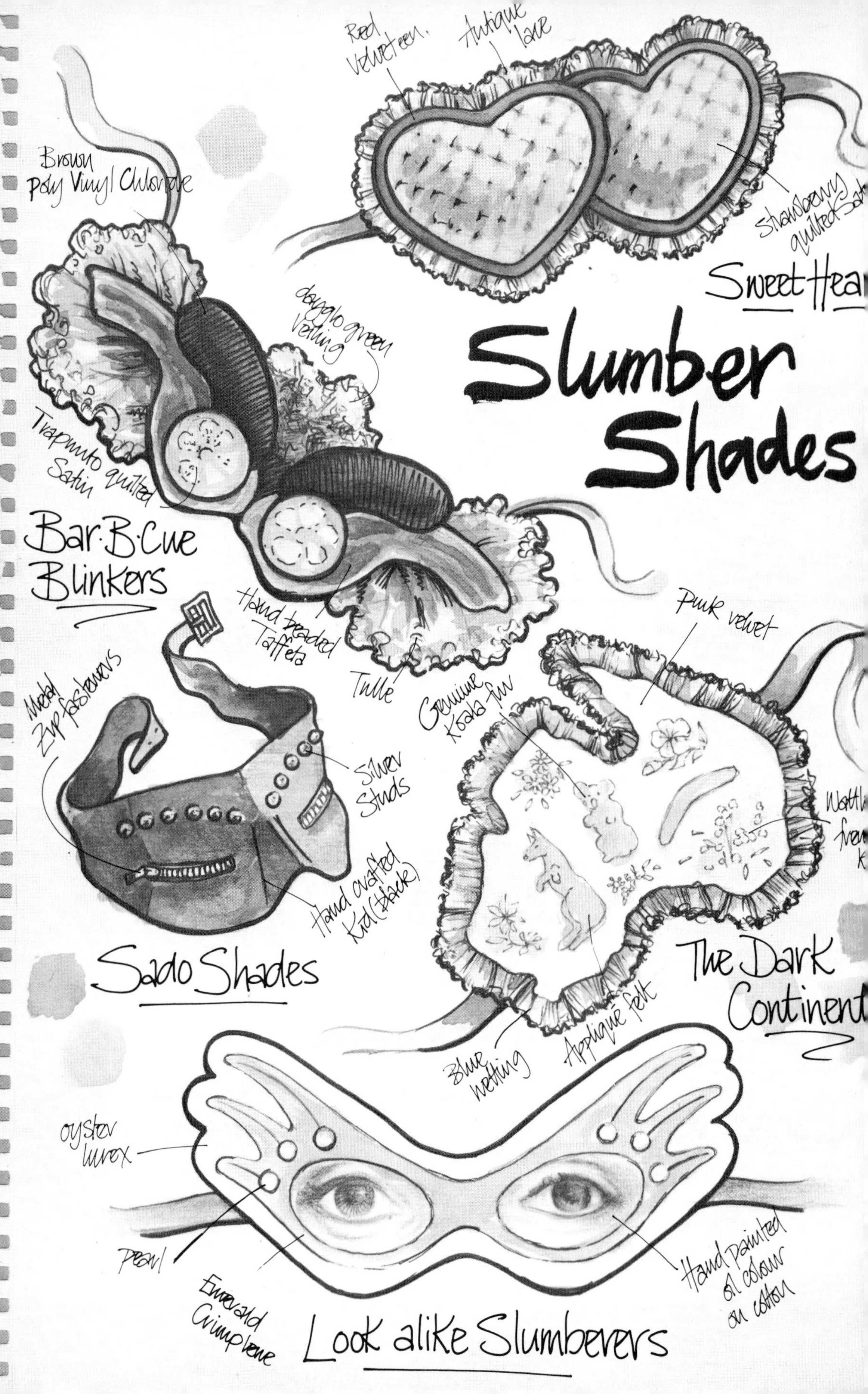

Red
Velveteen

Antique
lace

Brown
Poly Vinyl Chloride

Strawberry
quilted Satin

Sweet Hear

dayglo green
Vetting

Slumber
Shades

Trapunto quilted
Satin

Bar·B·Cue
Blinkers

Hand beaded
Taffeta

Tulle

Pink velvet

Metal
Zip fasteners

Genuine
Koala fur

Wattle
from
K

Silver
Studs

Hand crafted
Kid (black)

Sado Shades

The Dark
Continent

Blue
Netting

Appliqué felt

oyster
lurex

pearl

Emerald
Crimplene

Hand painted
oil colour
on cotton

Look alike Slumberers

AND SO TO BED

A LAID-BACK LOOK AT MAN IN REPOSE

Chances are you are reading this work tucked up in bed, though I tend to suspect that this is not the ideal publication for you to have your nose in if a bit of shut-eye is high on your list of priorities. Whether I like it or not, my company tends to be overstimulating, particularly at this time of the night. I'm sorry, but it is.

Chances are then, I tend to suspect, you have never bothered to study the history of the piece of furniture that supports you for one third of your life and – in the case of some of my readers – *all* their lives. (One of my computers tells me that I have a big bed-ridden 'following'.)

Being a bed-buff from way back, I made my nippers learn by rote the history of the happy home's most important piece of equipment. Our wonderful old Australian Aborigines always go on about 'The Dream-time', and their stunning old legends, passed on from mouth to mouth, are *all* about dropping off, having a snooze and generally putting your feet up at the end of the day. Believe it or not their idea of upmarket slumber is to be stretched out on a few goanna skins, bandicoot hides and wombat welts on a nice patch of dusty old outback.

I always told my bubbas when they woke up at night and asked for the umpteenth glass of water, that they'd be 'out amongst the Abbos' if I heard one more peep out of them, and it worked a charm.

The Ancient Greeks loved dropping off to music as I do. This little Peloponnesian pair are about to hop into the cot with a drum and a washboard. I pity their neighbours with that couple at it all night.

Peat dreams. This old sleepyhead nodded off in a bog a squillion years ago.

In Australia getting to sleep presents no serious problems providing bull-ants, webbos, vampire bats, death's head toads and other creepy-crawlies aren't on night shift, but the rest of the world over the millennia, has, I suspect, tried every blessed thing in the book to make their forty winks as cosy as possible. The Greeks, Romans, and early Brits stuffed all night long. Leather, rushes, straw, feathers and anything that came to hand to get their mattresses plump and snoozeworthy. Like the hippies and beatniks of today their beds were at floor level.

History does not tell us when the bed sprouted legs or when the great Herr Doktor Inner, of Innsbruck, masterminded what was eventually to bear his name, the innerspring mattress. With this invention sleep satisfaction took a giant leap upward.

Those of us who remember the old horsehair mattress of yesteryear and have heard senior citizens chewing the fat in terms of nocturnal restlessness, will have a pretty rough idea of what it is to plummet into the prickly gutter of a mule-mane mattress. Hence the warm greeting that was accorded Doktor Inner's springs.

But even the Herr Doktor's great gift to creature comfort had its teething troubles and when I was a kiddie our local tip was literally *teeming* with crumbling cast-off couches, perforated palliasses and done-for divans. Kiddies romping in the rubbish could see some pretty ropey gear that had gone the way of all flesh!

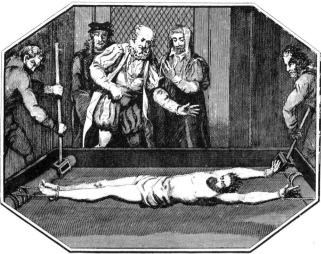

Here are a few sleep technicians of yesteryear putting an early orthopaedic bed through a rigorous testing programme. This same technique is used today, spookily enough, to discourage nail biting and other teenage habits.

Some of the shoe outlets of yesteryear must have been stunningly luxurious. This old etching depicts a corner of Mr Gucci's Oxford Street showroom. Note long-suffering salesperson (right).

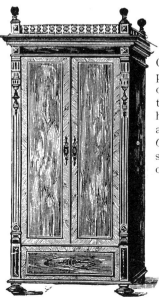

Closet bed. My son's business partner, Clifford Smail, said one of these had passed through his hands when he had his famous Australian antiques outlet, *Dead People's Gear*. This spring-loaded sleeper pioneered the concept of 'coming out of the closet'.

CHOOSING A BED

Being into Art Deco, I adored this mirrored number, but two of Madge is two too many.

You should always test a bed before you buy it, as Madge and I are in these pictures. I've always favoured a double bed because, spookily enough, if it hadn't been for my double bed my husband, Norm, might still be living at home. You see our early married life saw the advent of single beds, and although they have an obvious appeal for working women like myself, I hated the idea of having to reach across a horrid dark canyon in the middle of the night whenever I wanted to relieve myself with the nasal atomiser that Norm always kept in his jarma pocket. In those far off days I was pretty stuffed up most nights, though since I moved the vase of glads off the bedside table my nocturnal snuffles flew out of the window. Be that as it may. The nearness of Norm helped me to notice the first tell-tale twinges of the plumbing trouble that has since made his the most publicized prostate in the history of Western Waterworks. I'm convinced that if Norm had been popping up and down all night from his own single bed I might never have heard his prostate murmur and insisted that he had a first, second, third and fourth opinion on that naughty old rogue organ of his.

Many other medical opinions have flowed under the bed since then and my darling is at last in a single cot a long way from the luxury research assistant I'm dictating to now. My husband and I have cultivated acceptance of the fact that sneaking back into our queen-size double is not on Norm's list of options. Frankly I doubt if they'd get a fraction of his support system in the front door, let alone up my passage. *C'est la vie, Das ist kein los, hasta la vista.*

Daughter-in-law Joylene, trendy minx, once talked my fool-

Zing went the springs! Madge and I really punish mattresses – here's us girls trying the trampoline test.

Even a zillionairess can be shocked by a price tag – this one includes the Golden Gate Bridge and an Italian-designed brain scanner.

ish bridesmaid, Madge Allsop, into squandering her emolument on a water-bed. I'll never forget coming home to Everage Hall after an exhausting tour, to find Madge slithering around on a big bulging bladder of water in the middle of the bedroom that she and I had shared since Norm's last urethral thrombosis monstrosis.

'Get off that at once, you foolish wretch,' I cried, not realizing that my selfish old sleeping partner had also 'lashed out' on a new pair of stiletto sling-backs. I jumped out of the room just in time and my son Kenny's Olympus Trip 35 tells the rest of the sad story better than I can (see over the page).

I can't say I've seen the point of duvets. I always look at any-thing Scandinavian a bit sideways, and it's very hard to be properly tucked in with a stupid old duvet floating around on top of you. My wonderful old mother always used to lean over our beds after we'd said our prayers and tucked us in as snug as a bug in a rug, to use a wonderful old proverb of hers, and I must confess in this exclusive composition that I can't drop off these days until I've bleeped my chauffeur, Russell, who tiptoes into my pent-house, strips off his Gucci goatskin gauntlets, and with a whispered and sometimes even sherry-scented 'Goodnight, Dame Edna. Goodnight, Miss Madge' forces the blankets around us with his devoted digits. Then and only then, Possums, does this wide-awake, wizzie-headed workaholic nuzzle into a nook of Nepenthe.*

*Mature students and Open University readers don't need me to tell them that this is the name of an old Greek sedative from way back.

This gorgeous couch is a French invention...

but trust those artful old EEC folk to have a few saucy little tricks...

up their duvet!

Dame Edna's shopping extravaganza took place i
Maples, Tottenham Court Road, London.

THE NIGHT MADGE'S WATERS BROKE – Yours Truly to the rescue as usual. I imagine that tinted janitor's face is a picture – a 'pitcher' would be more useful in the circs.

A switched-on bed for a
switched-on Megastar –
my 'current' favourite.

Hot stuff! Yours Truly, the 'old boiler' – unlike
Madge Allsop I achieve everything under my
own steam.

Opposite A Laid-back Old Swinger.

EMPIRE HISTORICAL SOCIETY

DAME EDNA EVERAGE
Housewife Megastar slept here

Some Famous Places the Dame has Slept

The Dorchester, London
The Melbourne Hilton
Windsor Hotel, Melbourne
The Ritz, London
The Ritz, Paris
Mamounia Hotel, Marrakesh
Anne *née* Hathaway's Cottage,
Stratford-upon-Avon
Castle Howard, Yorkshire
The Mandarin, Hong Kong
Sacher, Vienna
The Elysée Palace, Paris
Parmelia Hilton International,
Perth
The Gellért, Budapest

Windsor Castle, Windsor
The Pierre, New York
Clarence House, London
The White House, Washington
Town House, Adelaide
Sandringham, Norfolk
10 Downing Street, London
Blenheim Palace, Woodstock
The Lodge, Canberra
Longleat House, Bath
The Royal Opera House, Covent
Garden
Buckingham Palace, London, by
social climbing, not drainpipe
climbing

MY PRESTIGE
VENUES

OR WHERE
NO-ONE
(BUT *NO-ONE*)
SLEEPS

BEDBUGS

I was sickened and horrified to learn from a scientific buddy that bed bugs are racist! Not that I've ever seen one or am ever likely to, heaven be praised, but my learned adviser tells me that *Cimex lectularius* is exclusively the white man's bed bug, while *Cimex rotundatus* likes to nibble tinted folk. Spooky, but true apparently, Possums. Personally I think this kind of discriminatory bugging of black and white beds should be stamped out.

These two species are wingless, parasitical, blood-sucking and foul-smelling. They can live for over a year without food and lurk in cracks in walls and floors and in the nooks and crannies of mattresses. Apparently DDT is the only thing to send them packing. Yuk!

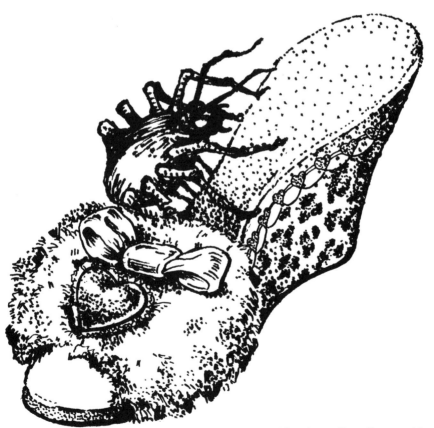

The Australian slipper spider (*Arachnida podophilia*), discovered by Helga Scholl, lives on dried talc and nail parings.

BEDSORES

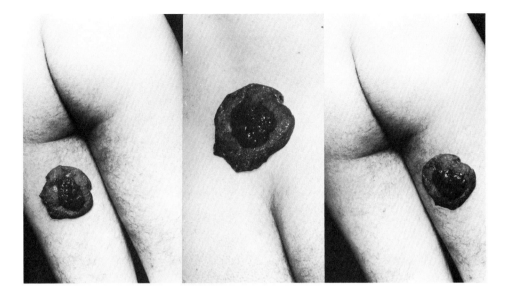

A bedsore is an eyesore in anybody's book, as my exclusive picture of an invalid's bottie shows all too graphically. Here is an old remedy that certainly worked on the cot cases in my family

DAME EDNA'S CUSTARD BEDSORE SALVE

Sponge patient every day after his bath with equal parts of methylated spirits and oil. Apply to back, elbows and any place where there is pressure. Dust with custard powder. If there is any soreness apply the white of an egg or lemon juice and put a pad of lint above and below the part to protect it.

THE SMAIL PATENT SNORE-CORSET

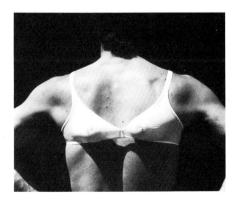

This brilliant idea of my son's flatmate, Clifford Smail, is modelled here by one of their friends. Apparently all the man has to do is to pop a couple of tennis balls into one of your old bras and wear it to bed back to front. I am assured this is an absolutely infallible cure for snoring

'in the wee wee small hours

I was thrilled to learn from my publishers that this book has been set as a standard textbook for Australian and UK final year Mothercraft nurses and social workers. It gives me joy to think that all my wonderful knowledge accumulated over the years as a mother and Megastar will be lovingly studied by students all over the world.

At a recent seminar on sleep, which I conducted in Sydney, many senior paediatricians quizzed me about bedwetting and its solutions. There are no easy answers. Nowadays bedwetting is seen as a largely psychological problem, but there is a long Australian tradition that mice have strong curative powers. Fried mice, preferably cooked alive, were a common remedy from early times, and the eighteenth-century housewife kept a quantity of cooked mouse ready for many medicinal emergencies.

I was once told by a well-known Melbourne sportsman and former Olympic athlete, who grew up in a rural district of Victoria at about the turn of the century, that during his childhood it was a common practice of some of the neighbouring families to serve their bedwetting children a portion of boiled mouse flesh as a preventative measure.

Luckily all my bubbas were potty trained from an early age, but here's a little exclusive. I was a very sensitive kiddie myself and in this deeply personal, no-holds-barred composition I'm going out on a limb as a fully paid-up card-carrying *bedwetter from way back*! My wonderful mother tells me she tried everything, including of course the famous Melbourne mouse-to-mouth method. And I'll never forget my darling climbing on to a chair and plugging into an electric light socket something attached to a couple of metal plates under my baby blanket. Whenever I get the call of nature in the middle of the night these days I miss the feeling of 2,500 volts creeping up my crevices. (Electrically minded readers may quibble with this voltage but when you're an incontinent kiddie who's counting?)

While on the subject of yukkiness here are a few ancient Australian recipes that my wonderful old grandmother swears by and which, spookily enough, she was thinking of putting in a separate book called:

CURE WITH MANURE
or
KEEP YOUNG WITH DUNG

Chances are this does sound a bit yukky, but jobbies play a big part in Australian folk medicine and my wonderful grandmother was a dab hand with the cow pats. Whenever Gran went down with anything, living in the bush as she did made it a lot easier for her to get her hands on the raw materials for some of these miracle kaa-kaa cures. Most medicines work best overnight and these are no exception.

WATCH POINT:

When applying a nocturnal cow pat poultice to any part of the body *whatsoever* make up the bed with old sheets that are nearly ready to go off to the Salvation Army. Your laundry won't thank you for a bundle of morning-after umber slumber-wear and it can be awkward explaining the cause of your blemished bedding, even to the most sympathetic laundress or dry cleaning outlet operative.

THE COW DUNG POULTICE

Remarkable results can be obtained from using the overnight cow pat poultice, not only in the case of boils and breast abscesses, but for bronchitis and pneumonia when no other remedy can be found. This is hardly yukky at all as the dung comes from the body of a ruminant who eats only grasses, herbs and gumleaves, so the dung – especially when hot and fresh – is perfect for dressings and, spread on clean linen and applied to the affected part, is as good as anything from the chemist.

COW DUNG CORDIAL

Press out the juice of the cow dung and sip slowly. This is an excellent remedy of yesteryear for bee stings and tumours.

HEN DUNG FOR SPARKLING EYES

Here is a beauty tip I have taken from Mrs E. Smith's book *The Compleat Housewife*, 1753. I haven't tried it yet, but I am convinced it would have gorgeous results, and I intend to try it on Madge's milky old orbs when she has her stitches out. Take the white of hen's dung, dry it very well and beat it to a powder. Sift. Blow it into the eyes on going to bed.

BOAR DUNG HOT FLUSH SPECIFIC

Another of Mrs Smith's overnight recipes is an excellent remedy for hot flushes. Take the dung of one boar. Pulverize it. Take it either inwardly or outwardly.
WATCH POINT:
Skulking around with a dustpan and broom in the vicinity of wild boars can sometimes be more dangerous than the flushes themselves.

MOUSE DUNG

This old English recipe is a wonderful end-of-the-day cure for little cuts that won't heal.

Take of mice dung beaten to a powder as much as will lie on a sixpence and put in a quarter of a pint of the juice of plantane (an old English herb) with a little sugar. Give it in the morning fasting and at night go to bed. Continue for some time and it will make whole and cure.

And last, but not least, here's an old Australian remedy.

BALDNESS-BALM

With mice fill an earthen pipkin. Stop the mouth with a lump of clay and bury within a manure heap. Leave for one year and take out whatever may be found therein. But it is urgent that he who lifts it have a glove upon his hand lest at his fingers' ends the hair come sprouting out.

NVALID BEDCARE

Thrill the bed-bound! Easy-to-follow, step-by-step instructions for a perfect 'hospital corner' Australian-style.

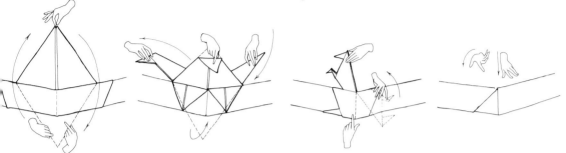

Here's an artist's impression of me doing a crash course in blanket bathing at the Royal Australian Prostate Foundation, of which I am life patron.

A detail of my husband Norm's prostate support system.

Great Australian Deathbed Declarations

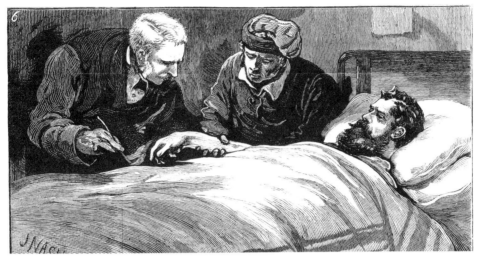

Ned Kelly said, 'I love Australia, I think.'

Australians are a thoughtful race of few words. It has been said that in my wonderful homeland 'the silence is eloquent'.

'Actions speak louder than words', was a priceless old proverb of my mother's and, spookily enough, her wise old words apply to the famous, if low-profile, Aussies listed below.

Here are just a few famous Australians' last words. Most of the other deathbed utterances that my research assistant dug up for me are generally about how wonderful it is to die in Australia, and I must admit people still flock there from all over the world with a view to passing away as quietly and comfortably as possible.

Let me confess in an exclusive for this book that I have sometimes wondered what *I* might say after a visit from the Grim Reaper. I can see myself in the wings of the gorgeous old spook-infested Theatre Royal Drury Lane, the sound of the audience clamouring for more echoing around my gem-encrusted lobes as my grief-stricken and inconsolable entourage, haggard with horror, strain to hear my last words from lips softly smiling in saintly resignation. Alas, I can also see Madge Allsop, aged one hundred and still going strong, thanks to the soft, cushy life my wealth has bought her, trying to give me mouth-to-mouth resuscitation through her latest set of cosmetic surgery dressings. No doubt in the dim, distant future when I am finally gathered by Dame Nature, my wicked bridesmaid will be hoping for the fiscal floodgates to open. My Swiss advisers have got a big surprise waiting for that wizened waif.

Anyway, what might I say when the last trump sounds and I sink into a bed of crushed glads? Frankly, darlings, I haven't the faintest idea. Probably something will come to me off the top of my head. *When hasn't it, let's face it?* However, I have had a spooky old hint from someone very close to a Certain Someone that, chances are, I'm not on Dame Nature's hit-list. In plain language – and don't get jealous – I just might go on forever. Can I hear my readers say 'Amen'?

Craig Moorhen, Hon. D. Lit. (Ho Chi Minh City),
Australian Short Story Writer and Chairperson of the Arts Advisory Board:
'Another cynical Arts cutback . . . the multinational bastards.'

Sir Keith Foley, Turf Broadcaster:
'What's the odds Doc?'

Sir Zoltan K. Prohaska, Architect NSW:
'I'm a personal friend of the Premier,
I don't need planning permission . . . Aarrgh!'

Dame Billie Butcher, Shot Putter:
'I'm chucking it in.'

The Hon. Alan Hopkinson, Statesman:
'Aw shit.'

The Joy of Tasmanian Sex

Whenever the subject of sex in the Southern Hemisphere pops up most thinking people think of Tasmania. In case your geography is a bit misty, it's a pointed little island nestling beneath Australia's exciting underbelly, and ever since they started sending eminent sex offenders there in olden days, satisfied honeymoon couples have helped to reinforce 'Tassie's' worldwide reputation as a respectable rendezvous for the raunchy.

Some of my best friends are Tasmanians, but quite frankly there are some spooky little nooks and crannies where the locals find it an uphill job choosing a mate outside the family circle. I'm sorry to have to say it between the covers of this tasteful book, but some of these more rustic rascals have been known to go through a *form of intimacy* with their immediate intimates, and the resultant off-beat offspring haven't thanked them either. In fact 'thank you' isn't in their vocabulary – they couldn't even spell it poor mites, loping through the bush and throwing crudely disfigured government issue family planning manuals at passing tourist buses, as sight-seers, with eyes like saucers, thunder past their perverse reserves.

Since the dusky inhabitants of Tasmania gave up the ghost many moons ago, Tassie hasn't any race relations problems. *Close relations problems* are about the only niggers in Tassie's wonderful woodpile.

Tasmania's cities are as modern as tomorrow, and the Powers That Be are always thinking of new ways of generating electricity to fuel the razors, hairdryers and teasing wands of tourists and Tasmania's powerful underground cryogenic plant. Every river, stream and rill has its own hydro-electric scheme and the Government is even installing miniature generators on taps in suburban gardens so that this wonderful isle is not thought to lag behind other less electrically minded countries.

On the domestic front, another notable feature is the encouragement that Church and State give to an old practice called 'bundling'. I've spoken to honeymoon couples who have visited some of Tassie's internationally acclaimed, award-winning, all-electric motels and have found to their surprise, and in some cases delight, a large plank or timber partition down the centre of their double bed. Finding the knot hole is Tasmania's answer to the Rubik Cube, and I'm told this splinter-prone pursuit has taxed the ingenuity of more than one Down-Under bundler. (This information, incidentally, had been fed to me by some of my computerized researchers and I'm only sorry that good taste prevents me from reproducing their pretty permissive print-outs in full.)

Bundling, incidentally, has also got something to do with going to bed wearing as many clothes as possible, and in the Tasmanian motels where this is compulsory you could sometimes spend a rather restless night, particularly if there is a fully operational hydroelectric plant whirring away in your en suite bathroom.

Whenever a Tasmanian sees a river he thinks in terms of instant damnation.

The off-beat Tasmanian practices that I have touched on in this fearless exposé will doubtless excite the world's curiosity as this wonderful book is translated into more and more languages. And, apart from the many social anthropologists like me, from foreign parts, who will want to quietly sit-in and scientifically monitor honeymoon couples and bundling parties, there will be a larger element homing in on my favourite island nook with only *one thing* on their minds. Unscrupulous sperm bank speculators (a new breed of cowboy on the modern fiscal scene) will see an opening in Tasmania for their underhand operations.

Go there while you can. Once the hard-nosed sperm bankers set up shop on every street corner you can kiss Tasmania's quaint old procreational preferences goodbye. The island will soon be full of heartbroken and redundant old uncles, cousins and disgruntled grandpas as the local lassies start shopping around for their nippers in deep freezers full of foreign fathering fluid. The Government has already let the sperm pedlars slip through its fingers, but it wouldn't surprise me if the Tassie authorities put up new barriers to stem the flow. Get in there quickly.

BED-IQUETTE

Once in bed, let's face it, Possums, we all make our own rules; 'horses for courses' as my marvellous mother once said off the top of her head. However, if you share your life and your sheets with a *special someone* there are a few teeny little do's and don'ts which, if observed, will make your bedroom a happier place. Here are just a few simple courtesies for the cot-conscious reader.

● If you are overnighting with a slumber-chum and his/her bedside phone rings, DON'T be tempted to answer it even with an assumed voice.

● If you are slightly disabled and staying in an hotel, DON'T leave your artificial limbs carelessly scattered around the room. Room service won't thank you if they trip over your fibreglass femur in the middle of the night.

● If you are a man, DO sleep nearest the door. In the unlikely event of a crazed rapist entering the room you'll be the first to learn of his intentions.

● DON'T read funny things in bed. There is nothing more irritating than trying to sleep while your slumber-chum cackles and falls about helplessly over, say, Bert Brecht's poetry, Monty Python, the new Erica Jong, or Buster Keaton scripts.

● DO always close your bedroom curtains before retiring. DON'T encourage sick high-rise voyeurs who love pointing their binoculars at careless cot-mates.

● If you eat in bed, DON'T plump for liquorice, lentils or hard-boiled eggs. It just needs one tiny spark of static electricity from an acrylic blanket and you and your pillow-pal could have an inferno on your hands.

● If you enjoy breakfast in bed, DO remember to sweep out all food detritus before re-making your bed. Your mattress-mate won't thank you if he/she leaps between the sheets and sustains serious skin lacerations from razor sharp Melba toast crumbs and back-chapping muesli.

● If you can't go to sleep without a digital, DO cover it with an undergarment. It's not much fun for your spouse watching those red numbers clicking by all night.

● DON'T point the foot of your bed towards the window. Old legends say this is just the opening vampires are on the look-out for, and, although I'm an old left-wing pragmatist from way back who doesn't believe in vampires, I'd rather be safe than sorry.

ARE YOU GOOD IN BED?

A QUIZ FOR COSMOPOLITANS

1 UPON RETIREMENT DO YOU
   a. *place your clothes neatly in the closet*
   b. *leave them lying on the floor higgledy-piggledy*
   c. *flop into bed fully dressed*

2 WHEN SAYING YOUR PRAYERS AT THE END OF THE DAY DO YOU
   a. *lock yourself into a kneeling situation at the end of the bed*
   b. *mutter a few selfish mumblings into the pillow*
   c. *don a negligee and accompany yourself on your boudoir Hammond organ in a selection from Carl Orff's gorgeous* Carmina Burana

3 DO YOU SEDATE YOURSELF WITH
   a. *prescribed drugs*
   b. *warm chocolate and malt-based beverages and herbal teas*
   c. *Tasmanian spider-web tablets*

4 IF YOUR SLEEPING PARTNER IS IN BED BEFORE YOU DO YOU
   a. *say goodnight by kissing him/her gently on the back of the neck*
   b. *wake him/her and give him/her a juicy smack on the chops*
   c. *lie quietly beside him/her all night and hope something happens*

5 WHAT WAKES YOU IN THE MORNING
   a. *a cock*
   b. *a digital alarm*
   c. *a cup of tea*
   d. *a combination of all three*
      (answer this carefully)

6 WHICH OF THESE EXOTIC BEDS WOULD YOU PREFER TO SLEEP ON

    a. A waterbed
    b. A futon
    c. A Shakespearean four-poster

7 WHICH OF THESE BEDS IS 'NOT ON' IN TERMS OF A SLEEPING SITUATION

    a. The Bed of Ware
    b. The Bed of Procrustes
    c. Diane de Poitier's bed

8 IN BED DO YOU WEAR

    a. pyjamas
    b. baby-doll shift, nightie, or mu-mu
    c. nothing but a pair of airline slumber-shades and a squirt of duty free

9 WHAT KEEPS YOU AWAKE AT NIGHT

    a. teeming insect life
    b. your husband/wife
    c. mental replay

10 HOW MANY SLEEPING PARTNERS DO YOU FAVOUR PER NIGHT

    a. one
    b. two–ten
    c. unrestricted

11 IF YOUR COMPANION ASKS FOR A DRINK DURING THE NIGHT DO YOU

    a. get one for him/her
    b. bite his/her head off
    c. pretend to be asleep

12 IF YOUR PARTNER SNORES DO YOU
  a. *wake him/her up and tell him/her to stop*
  b. *insert earplugs*
  c. *join in wholeheartedly*

13 IF YOU FEEL THE CALL OF NATURE DURING THE NIGHT DO YOU
  a. *slip into your en suite*
  b. *reach under the bed for a ceramic receptacle*
  c. *wait for it to go away*

14 BEFORE SLEEPING IN A STRANGE BED DO YOU
  a. *check out the sheets*
  b. *apply mild aerosol disinfectant*
  c. *forswear fastidiousness and snuggle in*

15 ON A COLD NIGHT DO YOU FAVOUR
  a. *a hot water bottle*
  b. *an electrified blanket*
  c. *the warmest thing that comes to hand*

16 WHEN WOOING SLEEP DO YOU
  a. *curl up in a ball*
  b. *stretch out on your tummy*
  c. *go to bed*

17 ONCE IN BED DO YOU
  a. *chat to your mate*
  b. *try to remember where you stopped reading Doris Lessing the night before*
  c. *politely initiate an act of gross immodesty*

*SEE HOW GOOD YOU REALLY ARE
BY TURNING TO PAGE 206.*

CROSSWORD

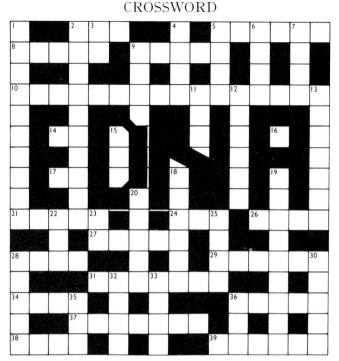

I've made this crossword a pushover, Possums, not to keep you up too late.

ACROSS

2 Bubba's bed *(3)*

5 I was raised in these ponds as a tiddler *(6)*

8 Sir Leslie Patterson could arouse this *(5)*

9 My pillow pal *(5)*

10 Florists know I'm one of these from way back *(9,7)*

14 My married name initially *(1,1)*

16 'Excuse ...?' *(1)*

17 English commuters exude this *(1,1)*

21 The last thing people do at my shows *(5)*

24 Call my macho son this at your peril! *(3)*

26 Famed Australian actor – not a Chink *(4)*

27 My husband's other support *(5)*

28 Joylene could turn a lovely home into one of these *(4)*

29 This glamour-puss is far in front *(6)*

31 Steep gods make paupers do this *(7)*

34 Affectionate diminutive for ebon nomad *(4)*

36 Backward housing for Eskimos *(5)*

37 The root of all beauty *(7)*

38 Pommie powder rooms *(4)*

39 I was this in my bridal bed *(6)*

DOWN

1 Dame Joan, Dame Birgit, little Dame Kiri and I are this *(10)*

2 Some marsupials are this in the end *(10)*

3 Former student of Melbourne Grammar School *(1,1)*

4 Beware these of Madge *(4)*

5 When it comes to stars I'm this sort, let's face it *(4)*

6 These tea-towel heads have us over a barrel *(1,1,1,1)*

7 I love to take a dekko at his work *(4)*

9 This slipper is a beast of burden *(4)*

11 See 24 across – another uncalled-for appellation *(3)*

12 The full extent of my husband *(6)*

13 Not exactly a hernia *(7)*

15 Most people's reaction to Mrs Allsop *(3)*

16 See 16 across *(1)*

18 My preferred marsupial *(6)*

19 The cultural centre of the world, let's face it! *(9)*

20 In India, I am this *(1,4)*

22 Scrummy but can't fly *(3)*

23 Rosemary Choate was my school's mistress of this *(1,1)*

25 I am this from way back *(4)*

28 Behind my son Kenny in everything he does *(5)*

30 I groove to this Horace *(5)*

32 Norm's title *(4)*

33 Whose shows would you rather go to any day of the week *(4)*

35 In short, my husband goes in for these *(3)*

36 Madge is a poor thing but mine ... *(3)*

(For a solution, see page 165.)

98

FLOWERBEDS

My Glads are gay and that's okay.

It's a spooky fact that flowers are just like people, in fact they're almost exactly the same except I suppose that people don't stand around all day in the dirt attracting bees. You can certainly think you know a particular flower for donkey's years without *really* knowing it, and it's amazing what our petalled pals get up to behind our backs.

I adore all flowers as you might expect, and being a pretty upfront, permissive Megastar from way back I don't mind what they do in the privacy of their own flowerbeds, or even vases, so long as they don't frighten the bumble bees or send the kiddies scampering indoors with eyes like saucers.

Rhodies, daffs, carnies, wizzie, phlox, stocks and hollyhocks are all gorgeous in my book, but most of my readers ought to know by now that I'm basically a one-flower female.

When I was burning my mother's things I stumbled across an old-fashioned, upmarket publication called *The History of the Gladiolus Australis*. I must say it was an eye-opener even to an old gladdy buff from way back like myself. The exciting facts in that old tome are stamped indelibly on my mind and I'll pass them on to you later in this composition if I can remember them.

Just in case you've never been to one of my wonderful flesh-and-blood shows, I should tell you that before the curtain falls I personally pelt my grateful audience with approximately in the vicinity of £500.00 worth of gladdies per night! Not many shows in the world do that. Let's face it, Possums – *none* do. These days you're lucky if you come out of a theatre with a smile on your chops, let alone clutching the moist stalk of a costly flesh-pink glad.

Embittered audience members emerging from meaningful and relevant shows in London's theatreland have often assaulted my laughing, gladdy-toting patrons in the street, seizing their floral emblems and making off into the night with them. Much good may my glads do these wretches, as they wither in milk bottles on grimy down-market window ledges. Mind you, you'd be lucky to get an Australian gladdy into a milk bottle without a good old dollop of Vaseline. I hope I'm not a 'size freak', Possums (I doubt if I would have tied the knot with Norm all those years ago if I had been), but, for the record, Australian gladioli make the English variety look like chives. I'm sorry but they do. In fact it always surprises me to see grown women gratefully grappling for them. However, it's an ill wind, and the miniature English glad has got a few pluses. When springtime comes you can at least sit out on the lawn and watch the daffodils and crocuses popping up all over the place without being sick with fear. In Australia, where I come from, no-one dares plonk themselves down in the garden like EEC folk can. In summer there are deadly funnel-web spiders and other creepy crawlies lurking with their mouths watering in the herbaceous borders and in the spring unsuspecting lawn-squatters run the terrible risk of being 'goosed' by an upwardly mobile gladdy. You see, Possums, in the fertile underbelly of my gorgeous subcontinent glads don't just drift to the surface like EEC crokes and daffs. Once the sun is shining and the flies are singing in the old garden gums, a batch of healthy stalks can thrust up so quickly that uninitiated sun-worshippers have been kebabed within an inch of their lives.

Old scholars agree the word 'Gladiolus' is a Latin word, probably invented by the Ancient Romans, so we can be pretty right in thinking the Romans must have visited Australia many moons ago, otherwise why would my wonderful subcontinent have the largest number of gladdies per capita in the world across the board at the end of the day? I'm pretty sure a nicer type of Roman, with green fingers, came to Australia, and I love to imagine them slipping out of their galleys and togas in Sydney Harbour and sneaking off into the bush to heel down a few corms. Archaeologists have dug up some of their old vases depicting Roman men and youths in their birthday suits getting up to a bit of hard-core botany. The Legionnaires' legacy is now one of the lesser known wonders of the Austral world.

Although it took them thousands of years, our wonderful aborigines were quick to see the possibilities of their native glad-forests, and not only did the macro-glads provide them with scrummy salads and timber, but weapons as well. My mother's old book contains a scarey mezzotint of an Australian Third World person giving an explorer a gladdy where it hurts most. Knowing as much as I do about the spooky side of this particular flower's history, I can hardly look at a vase-full these days without hearing the blood-curdling screams of missionaries and social workers of yesteryear being caught on the hop by a pointed floral tribute.

Round about the time when Oscar Wilde blotted his copy book, successful Arts Council grantees used to wander up and down Piccadilly Street, W1A 1ER, at all hours carrying gladdies and lilies for some reason or other. My son Kenny's informed flatmate, Clifford Smail, tells me that it was a bit like the modern fashion where young airline-ticket writers and opera designers have bunches of keys dangling on the belts of their jeans. Apparently (yukky thought) the Brideshead Brigade can send other members of the Brideshead Brigade uncalled-for messages just by jangling their Chubbs at each other. How sad to think there was a time when innocent glads were used as a semaphore of sickness.

The author potting

Yet how innocent are these raunchy old blooms? A chum of mine in the Botany Department of Melbourne University came up with some pretty scarey facts about the gladdy's sex life. Let's call her Dr Adrienne Clarke. No, on second thoughts let's call her Dr X because Dr Adrienne Clarke is her name. Dr X pioneered the research which found that my favourite flower is a *hermaphrodite*! I don't mind what glads do to each other in private, but little did I dream that some flowers, including my own *Gladiolus gandavensis*, actually did it to *themselves*.

At first I felt a bit sick. It's a jolt and a half when you learn that something you've loved and lived with for a lifetime is a, well ... a hermaphrodite. Naturally I had to look it up in my *Concise Oxford*, but, worse than that, I had to look at my vases thronged with sturdy stalks and say to myself: 'Edna, flowers need the light, they can't stay locked away in the closet all their lives.'

I'll never forget the shock I got when reading the ghastly news that Ms Anne Hathaway's cottage, where Shakespeare wrote some of his wonderful shows, had been looted. Priceless old crockery and cuckoo clocks, as well as pouffes and knick-knacks, had been souvenired by some unscrupulous teddy boys. I wonder if they checked the garden to see if any of Shakespeare's favourite shrubs were missing? Naturally my thoughts flew to Everage Hall in Moonee Ponds, Melbourne, with its roped-off uncut moquette armchairs and the ebb and flow of hushed pilgrims. What if the Hathaway connection decided to do-over my gorgeous shrine while I was trotting around the globe playing to packed houses and bringing joy to millions? Most vulnerable to predators is my famous garden where I keep some of the parent corms of my fabulous gladdy family. Criminal readers be warned that I have taken immediate precautions. Lay a finger on one of my bulbs and you'll know what 20,000 volts feel like.

KENNY'S BEDTIME FAIRY STORY

'Heavens!' I can almost hear the reader cry, 'Is there *no-one* in Dame Edna's talented family *not* wishing to rush into print?' Well, I've got to admit we are a little like Australia's Mitfords, Kennedys, Amises or Brideshead family, but I did not realize that darling Kenny's bent was literary till – on a routine search of his bedside closet – I came across a well-fondled, rather greasy typescript which I guess he never thought would see the light of day, but which I now proudly publish.

Of course, Kenny is very artistic and, with his background, I'm not surprised the fairy story was the *genre* he favoured, but heaven knows how he found the time to pen this offering.

Spookily enough, critics and linguists, the heroine of this story, *Edana*, bears a name that is an old form of my own and I think that the moral of the story – 'get with it' – could almost be mine as well! Doesn't that make you think, Possums?

The QUEEN'S NEW FROCKS

BY KENNETH MONTGOMERY EVERAGE

Once upon a time, many moons ago, in the backyard of the bijou palace of Organzika, there lived a pathetic little mite named Kennetta. Night and day she slaved away over her hot pedal Pfaff, for it was her lot to be Seamstress and Wardrobe Mistress to the court of Edana, Queen of all Organzika – and an outrageous old Queen at that.

Fashion was this particular Queen's passion and it ruled her life – and that of the good Organzikans. Even some of the days of the week were differently known in the Kingdom: Tullesday, Fursday and Satinday all had their own decreed fabrics that the populace were required to don.

Edana's waking hours were spent scanning the fashion pages of magazines from other kingdoms, or interrogating recently returned tourists on the trends they may have spotted abroad. Any fab fur or frock that caught Edana's eye was immediately confiscated for her *own* wardrobe.

For Edana was a terrific copycat and, as often as not, at dead of night the talented and put-upon little Kennetta was summoned to the Royal presence to shorten this frock, puff out the sleeves on that dress, trim this coat with sable and other upmarket schmutter. Kennetta was even required to act as Mistress of the Queen's eyewear – ensuring that the campy specs that the Monarch favoured to frame her eyes were suitably teamed with the Royal frocks.

Such endless nightly titivation finally got to poor Kennetta. To tell the truth she would rather have been in anyone's thrall than in Edana's. She often wished she could end it all and just drop off into divine everlasting dreams. She envied the Princess in that other fairy tale and the prick that put her to sleep!

But it was not to be. The only personage in the Kingdom that was allowed the luxury of dozing off for any period of time was Edana's swain, the King. And he spent *most* of his time unconscious while Edana cavorted and wassailed with her horny henchperson and confidante, Maid Madge (who still wore copies of her naff bridesmaid's gear by order of the Queen).

'Nod off?!' snapped Edana to Kennetta one day (for she could read Kennetta's thoughts). 'Come off it! Do me a favour! You were *born* with a mouthful of pins and that's the way I like it. Thou shalt stitch my shroud, child!'

And so it seemed it was to be. Kennetta was, let's face it, on a thread-mill. It was not surprising that she sobbed herself to sleep most nights and was depressed every waking hour. What particularly bugged her, was the total lack of job satisfaction. Sure, it was impressive to be the Royal Seamstress; but the thing that was a real downer for talented Kennetta was what passed for 'Style' in Edana's book.

For Edana could abide nothing raunchy or zappy: 'pizazz' was a foreign word to her. Edana was really into dumb pretty-pretty chockie-box beauty, even though it did *nothing* for her statuesque frame and classical bone structure. Organza, the national textile, and tulle – miles of it – were about as far as this nelly old Queen's imagination could run. She *swathed* herself in the stuff. Even when wind-surfing in the summer she trailed behind her yards of material that some whispered was a hazard to shipping.

One day she had the *whole of her kingdom* steam-rollered and buffed to a flat expanse so that no snags might catch her hemlines. This resulted in an even duller terrain for the Organzikan folk – and there was, of course, the constant danger of sequin storms.

As for Kennetta, she knew there had to be other 'looks' when it came to high fashion. Oftentimes she would sneak a look at the fab mode mags in the Palace Modethèque, before offending pages were stuck together by Maid Madge and her trusty glue-pot. In these divine pages she caught sight of alternative and, to her, alluring lines, mostly made up of a super material that she had decided was likely to grow on her.

'Let's face it,' she said to herself while Edana was out of thought-shot, *'I love leather.'* And she hugged herself with joy as she beetled back to her humble workroom.

And so Kennetta's thoughts began to dwell constantly on *tanned hides*. Her dreams were of knights in shining leather sweeping her away from Organzika and its humdrum fabrics.

The local people could not help but notice the transformation. Heavy-duty needles, twine and tooling devices started to be delivered to Kennetta's bijou showroom. But the Organzikans went on their way, in a froufrou of naff silk and bemusement, as Kennetta inwardly mocked and despised them.

Happily for Kennetta she *did* have some good friends – in the shape of the local fairies, a worldly lot who had between them chalked up a lot of flying time in their day. Their trad gauze and gossamer fairy uniforms made them feel completely at home in Organzika and caused little comment.

Every week Kennetta would run out to the fairy glen for drinks and to check out the fairies' gladrags. The members of this particular fairy circle were of all types and persuasions. As well as the rather 'trad' fairies – Ava, Susan, Rita and Jean – there were raunchier sprites – Liza, Barbra and the Bettes, to name but four. Judy was stunning, if always a mess, but perhaps Kennetta's favourite fairy was Mae, a real sport and always good for a giggle. Whenever Kennetta had to take this fairy's inside leg measurement for a pair of walk-shorts, Mae was sure to say, as the tape measure was unfolded: 'Come up and see me some time.' And all the other fairies would shriek with good-natured laughter as though they'd never heard it before. Such was the bonhomie and good-vibes situation that reigned at the Organzika Dell.

So it was not surprising that when, one day, Kennetta

fronted up at the dell feeling rather tacky and down in the mouth, the good fairies noticed. Judy stopped pushing her trolley, Bette and Joan stopped spitting at each other, and they all gathered around. As the Head Fairy, Mother Marlene, interrogated: 'Was ist los, liebchen?'

'All this tulle is getting to me,' sobbed Kennetta, her stunning eyes red-rimmed from weeping and late-night titivating, her tacky hair bespattered with naff sequins and her stubby, overworked fingernails engrained with glittering bead fragments.

'I really long for leather. That's where it's at,' she literally spat out as the fairy band looked on pityingly.

Joan sprang forward instantly, waving a coathanger, her mouth a slash of crimson. 'We've *got* to do something about this nelly old Edana; I agree with Kennetta. And I have a plan.'

The fairies moved closer as Joan went on. 'I'm pretty well in with Maid Madge,' she said as the fairies exchanged knowing nudges and winks, 'and she has Edana's ear.'

'Oh, how generous of Edana,' piped up a fairy named Marilyn. 'I know Madge is heavily into implants and so on, but . . .'

Again all the fairies shared a chuckle, but this did not put Joan off her stroke for a moment.

'One of Madge's more straightforward duties is as Librarian – vetting all the mags and videos that come in to the Palace for the juicy bits, so that Edana doesn't have to waste her time finding them herself to decide if her subjects should have access to them. I'll ask Madge to tear out, or record-over, any naff pro-pretty fashion puffs and so brainwash Edana away from all that soft stuff. Meanwhile, with our magic powers we can cast a spell on the menfolk of Organzika so that whenever they see or touch organza, tulle, silk, satin and related smooth schmutter, they are sick to their stomachs. On the other hand, when they behold or stroke leather or other bona gear, they shall be mightily aroused. As you know, Madge's surgical sutures are made from the finest cowhide, so she will play along with us, and doubtless soon find herself the object of men's desires as never before. Edana will freak with jealousy and marvel what is Maid Madge's magic.'

The fairies threw up their hands in admiration for Joan's plan and opened some vintage Pepsi to celebrate.

Kennetta returned to her studio, grateful for the fairies' understanding and still smiling at darling Mae's 'finishing touch' – to throw down tacks in front of Edana at the following day's procession so that her organza, tulle, etc., would be snagged and the Queen's ensemble would hardly last the course due to its raggedness.

'Then Edana will be truly tacky,' said Mae with a twinkle in her eye.

The next day dawned – Organzika's National Day, Tullesday the first of Tulle-eye – and the populace was assembled before the palace for the procession to the *unbelievable* Organzikan national shrine. As usual, Edana sashayed out from the Royal dwelling without her husband, swathed (but swathed) in every kind of campy luxurious raiment smooth to the touch.

But instead of the usual appreciative gasps there arose a manly full-throated 'Yuk!' from the crowd. Edana naturally assumed this reaction was to Maid Madge, who walked a few paces behind her; but her eyes behind her spectacles flashed when she heard the next mass utterance.

'Make mine a Madge', and such-like calls mingled with wolf whistles as the Maid made her way.

Edana wasted no time. She turned to the faithful wench, grabbed her and pinned her to the ground.

'Not now, Edana,' wailed the poor waif, but Edana was all over her like a rash, magnifying glass in hand, prying into every nook and cranny, searching for the source of her attendant's new-found sex appeal. So rough was her man-handling of Madge that several hide stitches came undone. Some wrapped themselves around Edana's throat, giving the appearance of a makeshift necklace. Others entangled her wrists like bracelets.

A hush fell on the crowd. Then the menfolk surged forward. 'Edana the beauteous! What a brilliant Queen!' were some of the more acceptable cries that now reached Edana's ears. Edana's old eyes never missed much, and immediately she cottoned on to the leather accessories story as the cause of this swelling admiration. Seizing a stunning saddle from one of her horse guards, she strapped it to her person. Madge's (admittedly) leatherette serviceable handbag became an instant and freaky piece of headwear. Edana hitched up her frock to expose her spunky leather shoon and, with each new movement, the excitement grew. Some of the yells were, of course, due to Mae's fairy tacks, which were beginning to take their toll. But this mattered not to Edana, and would not have mattered had she known it.

Kennetta could hardly believe her eyes as her firmly favourite fabric seemed to take over the event. She was yanked bodily from the fray and given her orders by Edana to get back to her bench and run up a *complete new wardrobe* for that evening's festivities.

And from that day on leather reigned supreme and all the tacky old-fashioned frills and bows were banished from Organzika where the people – and the fairies – lived zappily ever after.

There was an old man of Pompeii
Whose pyjama elastic gave way
As his dress he adjusted
Vesuvius busted
And here's what he looks like today.

MADGE
MY MIRACLE MASSEUSE

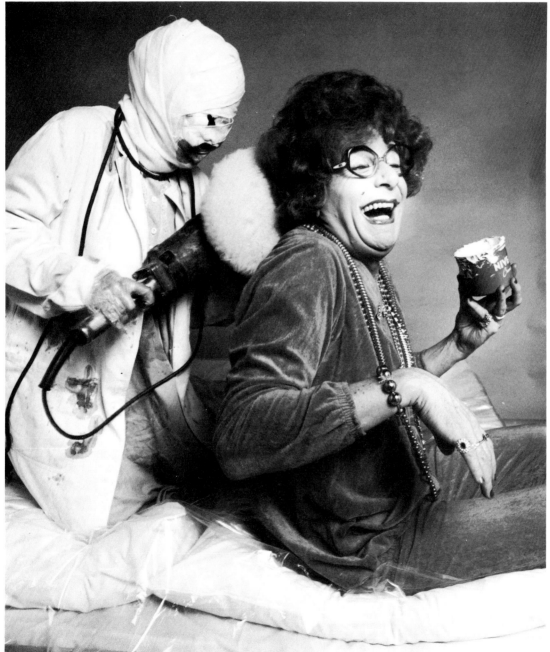

Mmmm . . . Madge!

Ugh!

Ouch!

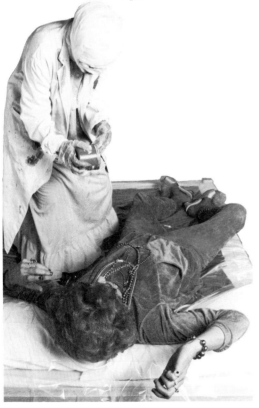

Squelch.... Go easy darling!

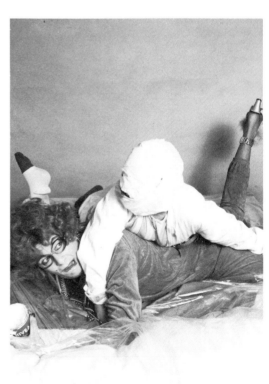

What are you up to woman?

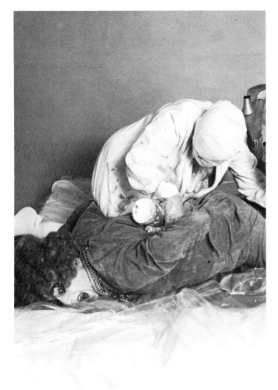

You brute!

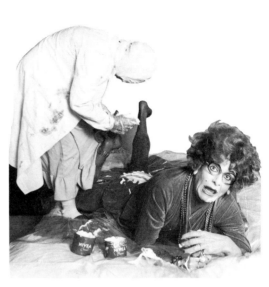

You said it wouldn't hurt.

Enough is enough, I've got a headache.

Not there, you foolish wretch.

Not *there* either!

I asked for massage, not massacre.

Give me that Nivea!

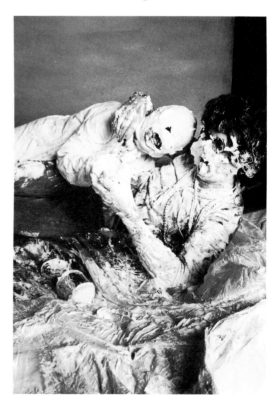

You were so firm but gentle.

Eat your heart out Francis Bacon.

ACT I   ACT II

WORKSHOPPING AMADEUS

Madge and I in two exciting scenes from the wonderful musicale *Amadeus*, presented by the Woolloomooloo Women's Drama Workshop at the prestigious Theatre up the Wall and subsidized by a generous government grant. In these dramatic pickies you can see me really getting into the role of Salieri, while Madge barely copes with the stupid part of Mozart. (Nominated for a Golden Goanna.)

POOLSIDE
PLATTER

Parma Koala **Platypus du Jour**

Nivea Toast **Marmite de Vegemite**

beauty counsellor's case book

first I boosted her morale

on the road to beauty

How to look like me

Will the real Dame Edna 'ease stand up!

BONJOUR

*mes possums from moi
et mon entourage à la*
LEVÉE de L'EVERAGE

Bedibles

Midnight Snacks–
Witching Hour Wonders

GREEN FIRE – FOR THE JADED PALATE

INGREDIENTS

1 tin of asparagus
1 egg
1 tsp tabasco or chilli sauce
grated cheese
seasoning

METHOD

Mash the asparagus, after removing from the tin. Blend with chilli sauce, pepper, salt, grated cheese and whipped egg. Stir over a high flame until the mixture starts to phutt and curdle. Pile on buttered, slightly burnt toast and serve.

      If your menfolk have come home late after a convivial evening with their colleagues and/or peer group, this piquant snack always goes down very well. Make sure they remove their ties when eating it as it can leave very yukky exorcist-like stains on clean haberdashery.

YIELD: ONE PALATE–TINGLING DISH

LIZARD ISLAND OMELETTE DE PINEAPPLE
À LA JOHN GORDON

(A favourite of my maître de danse.)

INGREDIENTS

3 tbsp melted butter
3 beaten eggs
3 tbsp drained crushed pineapple
4 strips crisply fried fish-fed bacon
2 oz cream cheese, cubed

METHOD

Heat Teflon omelette pan at high temperature until slight vapour appears.

Pour in melted butter. When butter stops bubbling, add eggs and shake pan rapidly in a circular motion. When omelette is set but still slightly soft in centre, slide on to heated plate and spoon pineapple into the centre. Add fish-fed bacon and cream cheese and fold omelette in half. Serve. The Lizard Islanders lap up these luscious midnight mouth-pleasers.

HONOLULU BLACK PUDDING

Apparently 'black pudding' sausages are not as yukky as they sound and are made only from the nicer parts of a dead animal's blood. In spite of this they've never slipped very easily down *my* red lane. Nonetheless here is a scrummy recipe that I have tested successfully on the odd loved one.

INGREDIENTS

1 can pineapple rings
1 black pudding sausage
egg batter

METHOD
Thickly slice the black pudding, one slice to a pineapple ring. Trim sausage circles to fit pineapple holes. Dip in a good egg batter. Deep fry in peanut oil.

The batter holds the sausage centres in place and surprisingly enough this dish can be served with peppermint and chocolate chip ice cream if your loved one is really peckish.

YIELD: VIVID TROPIC DREAMS

SLUMBERTIME SNACK

INGREDIENTS

6 mashed, large over-ripe bananas
½ cup water or apple juice
3 tbsp raisins

METHOD
Put mashed fruit in heavy saucepan with juice or water and raisins. Heat gently. Stir constantly for about 5 to 10 minutes or until the fruit is completely cooked. A gentle dish, excellent for before-bed snacking.

BILLIE JEAN'S NANA-FURTERS

(Given to me by a little chum in the sports world.)

INGREDIENTS

I medium size tin of pineapple chunks
½ cup chopped onion
½ cup finely sliced celery
I beef oxo cube
I tbsp cornflour
I tbsp brown sugar
2 tbsp cider vinegar
I tbsp soy sauce
½ lb plump, juicy frankfurters, sliced into rounds
4 larger ripe bananas, sliced into large chunks

METHOD

Drain pineapple and reserve syrup. Melt margarine in saucepan, add onion and celery and cook until tender but crisp over a low flame (about five mins). Dissolve oxo cube in boiling water. Combine cornflour, brown sugar, vinegar, soy sauce, and reserved pineapple syrup. Add oxo and pour over cooked onion and celery in saucepan. Cook, stirring until mixture thickens. Add plump juicy frankfurters, pineapple chunks and bananas. Heat through, stirring to prevent sticking. (Serve on a bed of mashed potato garnished with fresh parsley.)

YIELD: NUMMY NANA-FURTERS

FIJI FRANKIES – A SCRUMMY VARIATION

INGREDIENTS

¼ cup apricot jelly or plum jelly
¼ cup finely chopped favourite bottled chutney
I¼ tbsp cider vinegar
pinch of garlic salt
14 oz tin of plump, juicy frankfurters
2 firm bananas cut into rounds.

METHOD

Prepare in frying pan by mixing jelly with chutney, vinegar and garlic salt. Add plump, juicy frankfurters and bananas, heat thoroughly, stirring constantly. Serve hot over mashed potato. Use small forks.

BRECHT-FASTS

I often try to imagine what my very favourite people would have started the day with. Sylvia Plath, Tolkein, Anaïs Nin, Orson Welles, Rosa Luxembourg, and of course Virginia. What did these wonderful women of history tuck into before getting the kiddies off to school and plugging in the Hoover?

I tend to suspect that Bert Brecht (one of my very special people) never wrote any of his delightful ditties on an empty stomach. Since history tells us he was of German extraction chances are sausages and sauerkraut were top of the menu and I must say in winter I myself adore a sausage breakfast.

SAVOURY AUSTRALIAN CHILLIED SAUSAGES À LA BERT BRECHT

INGREDIENTS

pork sausages	*seasoning*
chilli powder	*flour*
onion	*stock*

METHOD
Select nice firm, plump pork sausages and boil until tender. Fry onion and chilli powder, season, add stock, water and a little flour to thicken. Slice the sausages and cover with sauce. Serve on a bed of rice, garnished with chutney or apricot jam.

YIELD: ONE SCRUMMY BREAKFAST

PORK 'N ZOLA

A spooky old medium once told me that Ms Plath, the poet of yesteryear, adored watching me cook from the astral plane. Especially this scrummy breakfast recipe for pig's trotters. Little Sylv was even writing a poem about me so my occult adviser, Hepsibah Watkins, informs me, beginning

I love to watch Dame Edna cook
Even though I'm just a spook.

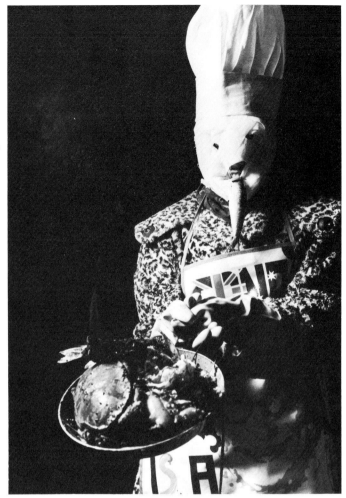

Madge's morning after fritto-misto. My economy-conscious bridesmaid frying up my fishy facial.

I'm not a superstitious woman, in fact I'm an old left-wing pragmatist from way back, but I must say that uncanny little poem sold me on the idea that old Sylvia was still up there somewhere bashing out some pretty useful and confrontative hexameters.

   Select some nice trotters but make sure your little butcher only sells you the front ones, or a pair as far away from the yukky end of Porky-boy as possible. Give them a good old-fashioned pedicure and marinate overnight in a dettol solution (your menfolk won't thank you if their fortifying breakfast is quickly followed by a terminal bout of swine fever or Atkinson's sty rot). Steam your trotters, allowing one for each person, until the meat is pulpy and quilted. Serve as imaginatively as possible with gorgonzola bechamel sauce. Finish off with a decorative banana garnish and watch the menfolk's faces.

YIELD: ONE DISH OF PORK 'N ZOLA

WATCH POINT: NOT RECOMMENDED FOR RED SEA PEDESTRIANS

THE BED
IN ART

Although I'm an old left-wing pragmatist from way back, I've got a spooky feeling there's something in Reincarnation after looking at these great masterpieces of yesteryear. Sometimes I wake up in the wee small hours feeling as though the whole Royal Academy has had a dab at me.

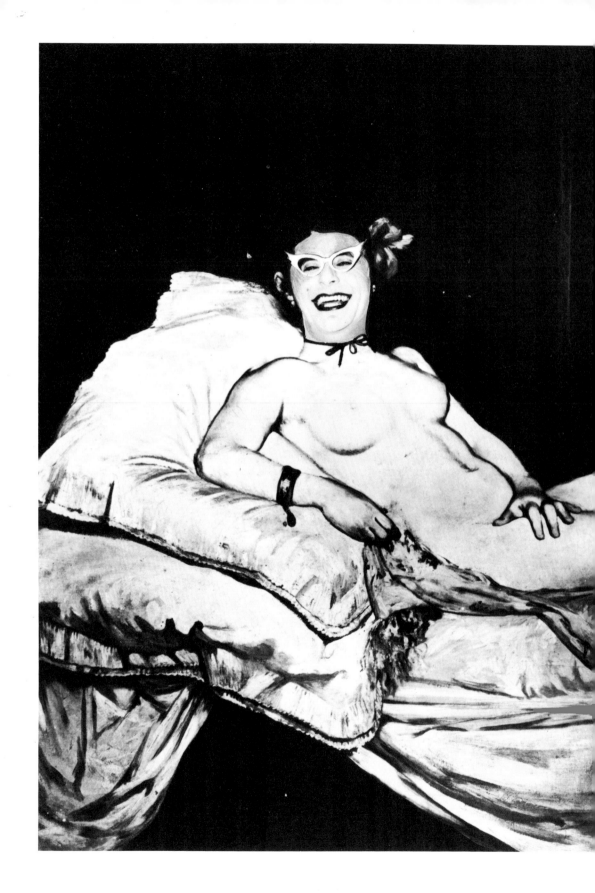

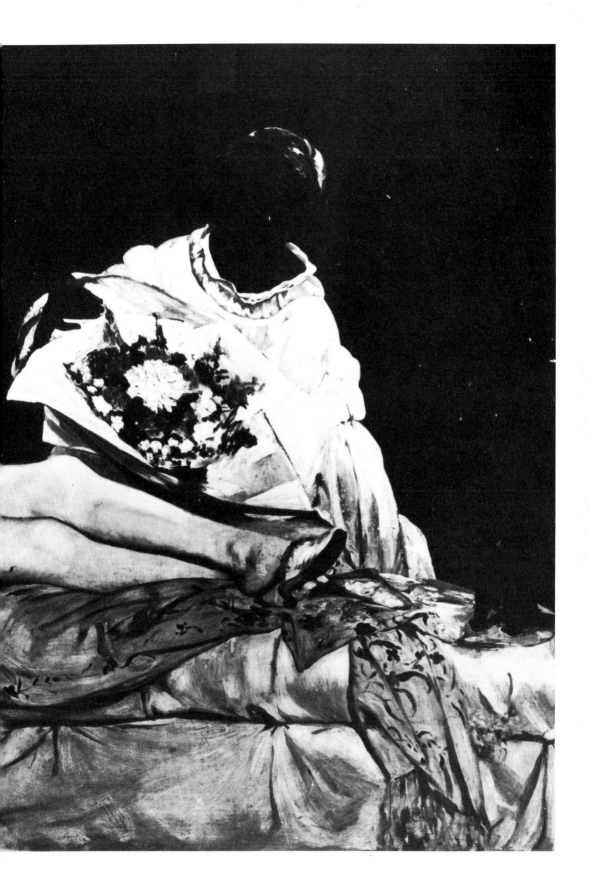

DECO DAME

These pickies show Madge and me shuffling around a tiny corner of my stunning, comprehensive and pivotal collection of *objets d'art*. My poor bridesmaid always gets very excited by one particular nook in my extensive holdings. The silly old duffer even calls one of my priceless paintings 'Edna and Madge'. Chance would be a fine thing. The cultured man in my fourth snap is Big Vic my art adviser, bijoux custodian and part-time 'heavy'. No-one crosses Big Vic and lives to tell the tale. 'What's this got to do with bed?' I can hear you say. Cultured readers and Kenny's friends will have noticed that in a number of pictures in this volume I'm propped up against the most priceless example of Australian Deco in any hemisphere.

MY BIRTHPLACE

This old Australian pioneer cottage was destroyed by floods, bush fires and snakes many moons ago, but it is on this historic spot that my wonderful parents brought me into the world. Of course it doesn't look like this today. For that matter would Shakespeare recognize Anne Hathaway's cottage if he went there now? Not likely. Anyway this humble little patch of Australian soil is now a national shrine and worked-up pilgrims from all over the Australian-speaking world are often treated by trained nurses as they queue round the clock to glimpse my memorabilia. This old-fashioned daguerreotype shows my wonderful gran standing on the front porch with the entrance hall-cum-foyer behind her at her rear. On the left is the en suite bathroom where my marvellous mother was first potty trained. Oh that those early lessons did not now require daily reinforcement at the hands of Matron Totentanz at Dunraven, St Peter's Close, Melbourne, where Mummy is now a pampered guest.

There's a wonderful proverb my mother once said:
'If you want to know someone, look under their bed.'

137

MADGE'S SIDE   MY SIDE

EDNA DEAREST

One evening recently, in the middle of the night, a world-famous publisher gave me a tinkle out of the blue. Let's call him Lord Nicolson. His voice seemed tense. 'Something has come into my hands which I have to show you Edna,' was all he said. 'Can you lunch with me at the House of Lords tomorrow?' Mystified I agreed, and the next day I met the good Lord at our *Art Nouveau* rendezvous.

Over lunch I noted the lines of tension that creased his face and his Savile Road suit, and I wondered when he would come to the point. It was then Lord Nicolson gravely passed across the coffee cups a slim manuscript in prematurely childish typewriting. 'We've been offered this book,' he said huskily. 'It's probably the hottest literary property of the eighties, and there isn't a publisher in the world who wouldn't pay big bickies upfront for the hardback rights, world paperback deal, topping-up option and serialization across the board per se, at the end of the day.'

I peered at the Peer. What was he trying to tell me? 'It's written by someone very close to *you* Edna,' he said in a hoarse whisper. 'A sick and troubled little girl, but it's a hot property all the same.'

Quickly I perused the stained manilla covers for some clue to the mystery, and as I did so I felt as though an icy hand had gripped my tummy. The blood drained from my famous face, I felt sick and giddy, and it wasn't the poached salmon that I had just enjoyed with my peer group either.

Lord Nicolson's bombshell was written by Valmai Gittis, *my only daughter*.

Who knows how long I sat there turning page after pitiful page. Only a caring, loving mother reading this can know how I felt as my Val emerged from the pages of her book a monster of ingratitude, biting the hand that had changed her nappies. Time must have stood still as the pages drifted like autumn leaves from my lap on to the floor and the stewards were already setting the tables for dinner as I came to the end and looked up for the first time to see my eminent friend asleep in his chair, somehow older, greyer.

I was speechless, which is unusual for me. What words any-way could express my anguish and, yes, anger. If she ever did get some publisher to print her disturbed twaddle who would ever believe it? Yet at the same time I recalled full well that my beloved homeland of Australia was chock-a-block full of jealous pygmies who love to chop the heads off tall poppies and who would like nothing more than to see me humiliated by the feckless fruit of my womb.

It was as though Lord Nicolson read my thoughts as he

dropped me off at the Dorchester in his Rolls. 'No decent publisher will touch it Edna,' he reassured me. 'But they'll print it in Australia all right, and they'll pay big bickies across the board at the end of the day. I hear Rupert's already put in a bid.'

'No they won't.' I suddenly cried defiantly. '*I will*. I'll publish it myself. I'll publish Valmai's so-called autobiography at my own expense and include it in my next bestseller, *Dame Edna's Bedside Companion*. Let everyone read what this wicked waif has to say. Let my millions, no, zillions of readers judge me *then*.' Lord Nicolson gasped, 'I knew you were plucky Edna,' he said, 'but in all my years of kicking around the traps of the publishing industry I've never struck such sheer bloody bravery across the board at the end of the day. Good luck. God speed.'

It *was* the end of the day and as I tottered into the arms of Madge Allsop (after a security man had withdrawn), the built up tension of the day climaxed in a flood of hot salt tears. Somehow, my tousled wistaria head cradled in the knees of my understanding, if foolish bridesmaid, I blubbed out the incredible story – *my* side of the story.

'Someone's put her up to it,' was Madge's first remark when she saw the whole sick scenario – oh how I wished that were true. If I ever find that person I'll make her life a living hell. 'Sticks and stones will break your bones but autobiographies will never hurt you', was one of my wonderful mother's sayings – or words to that effect.

You be the judge now, darlings. I loved Valmai, I still do. She's far from a well type of person. Medical men with bleepers who I adore will read this and agree with me. My daughter needs help, that's what this autobiography is all about – a cry for help.

I'm only printing an extract because it would make everyone sick if I reprinted it all. I'm sorry but it would.

Val, do your worst.

'This is the hottest property I've ever handled,' he ejaculated.

EDNA DEAREST

The nice staff have given me some paper and a little typewriter
and loosened this silly jacket around my arms.
'Why not let it all hang out, Valmai,' said one of the doctors
through a long tunnel. That's what I'm doing. Oh the relief,
the relief!

At Moonee Ponds Polytechnic the kids used to really suck up to
me , the girl with the Megastar Mum. Mind you she wasn't a
Megastar then, but when Mummy won the Melbourne Lovely
Motherhood Contest back in the rock 'n rolling fifties it was
a big deal. I guess I felt kind of proud too because she was
beautiful, and still is let's face it, whereas I was a loner,
an ugly duckling.

One terrible day Dad took us kids aside. There was me, Brucie
and little Kenny.
'Your mother's had a wonderful offer to go up to Sydney in a
show with Barry Humphries. She's always wanted to tread the
boards and this is the chance of a lifetime for her to work with
the most talented man ever born in the Southern Hemisphere. We've
got to let her go kids, so she can get it out of her system.'

What our darling Dad didn't tell us or Mum was that Dr Polkingho
had just given his prostate six months at the outside. The next

day ~~as~~ we stood at the front gate of the old Moonee Ponds home and saw the woman who had cuddled us, heard our prayers, our hopes, our fears, step into Barry Humphries' limo and drive out of our lives.

STUPID DUFFER!!

Soon after that I married Mervyn Gittis and Mum managed to fit our wedding into her tight schedule, but she was a changed person even then. No longer wearing simple frocks and flatties, she appeared in a peacock and cyclamen Thai silk confection. All the women clucked around her, examining her new upmarket brooches and posh accessories. The bride was well and truly upstaged, to use a showbiz expression.

NOW SHE TELLS ME

Somehow Mervyn and I have never been able to use the 'Cries of London' dinner mats she gave us. What relevance did they have to our lives, living as we did in Melbourne in the second half of the twentieth century? The thing that nearly broke my heart that day as she swep' off to catch her plane back to Sydney was to see the way she kissed Dad. Instead of a juicy smack on the chops she gave him a chilly little peck on both sides of the face, like a glamour puss in a continental film. On my wedding night I cried myself to sleep in Merv's winceyette arms. I may have gained a husband but I'd lost a mother.

MEN BOOZE AND DRUGS

TWADDLE!!

After I'd had the first of my little ones the headaches ~~and thos~~ and the nightmares started. Merv was so gentle yet firm as he led me caringly back to the bedroom of the unassuming triple-fronted, cream tapestry brick veneer that my famous mother had given us in one of her impersonal acts of 'generosity'.

'You've been sleepwalking again, that's all, Valmai darling,' he'd say.

'Did I talk in my sleep Mervyn? Did I say anything we can tell Dr Emanuel at the next family therapy session?'

'Just what you always say Valmai."Don't leave me Mummy, don't leave me!"'

When Wayne was born, Mummy was performing in Melbourne. By this time the Australian critics were using adverbs like 'international acclaimed' and 'award winning', expressions that they never use lightly. Dad had had the first of his operations and guess what, Mummy was really playing for sympathy. Know what I mean, the full broken-hearted clown scenario bit, the whole 'show must go on' trip. Get it? Anyway Mum came along to the christening with a truck-load of pricey presents. BIG DEAL. And a form saying Wayne had been enrolled at Melbourne Grammar, the elitist school that has turned out some of Australia's top Insurance Brokers and upmarket Motor Dealers. As the Bahai celebrant dipped Wayne's head in the scented oils I guess I blew my top. Mum as per usual looked georgeous, chatting up my old friends from Uni and twisting Mervyn round her little finger as per usual.

By the seventies Mummy was really big time in the UK, and we saw even less of her. She had a telex put in next to Dad's bed, but did she teach him how to use it? <u>Do me a favour! Come off it!</u> She also opened a Swiss bank account for him. Fat chance Dad would ever be allowed out of hospital let alone on a pair of skis. Clever Mum. <u>Bloody clever. Ace, Game and Set!</u>

Sure she pulled a few strings and my husband got promotion. What was I expected to do? <u>Grovel</u>?!

SHE COULDN'T SPELL THANKYOU

My big brother Brucie moved inter-state. He was the strong silent type, but I saw the anguish on his face when Mum started making value judgements about his wife Joylene in public. Even on the stage.

KINKY FROLICS

I've lost count of the number of times I've been put away for a rest on trumped-up excuses, nicked in shops and supermarkets, usually with gear planted under my kaftan by creeps hired by Mum more than likely. God knows I've never threatened <u>her</u> career. <u>DO I HAVE TO READ MUCH MORE OF THIS?</u>

It freaks me to think she wants me locked away. A lot of Doctors and Social Workers I've met reckon I could have been a great actress. Is <u>that</u> what Mum's scared of? Another Megastar in the family? She'll deny it sure, but my Karma is never wrong. They gave me some funny pills the other day and I remembered something I must have pushed to the back of my mind. I was a kid. Dad was away having the first of his prostate exploratories and Auntie Madge had moved in after Uncle Doug's accident at the mud springs in New Zealand. I guess I cried myself to sleep that night as per usual, <u>so what's new?</u> Come off it. Sometime in the night I got up for a midnight snack and as I was passing Mum and Dad's quarters I was freaked to hear some really weird grunts and squelching noises. I was a curious kid and I'm even more curious now. So I guess I peeked through the slightly open door which was ajar. I hope no kid reading this ever sees her mother doing what I saw Mum doing with Auntie Madge and a jumbo jar of Nivea cream. Sure Mum **always** had a stiff neck but did Aunt Madge have to start at her ankles. PULL THE OTHER ONE.

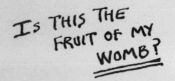

Is THIS THE FRUIT OF MY WOMB?

MY BROTHER A PANSY

But it was what she did to Kenny that hurt. He was <u>always</u>
artistic. More than one Australian critic said he had international
acclaim and award-winning potential, and let's face it they're
not the kind of adverbs Australian critics chuck around. Pretty *SICK*
soon Mum sent for Ken, who had dropped out of his design course *SICK*
and had started drifting from job to job. You know the scenario. *SICK*
He was trainee Qantas steward, a contemporary dance choreographer,
an Adelaide Arts Festival Comptroller, and a P&O cruise co-ordinator
As far as Ken was concerned butter wouldn't melt in Mum's mouth.
So when she snapped her jewelled fingers he zotted over to London
as Mum's number one groupie. And did he say goodbye to his father
in the Urological Unit? A likely story. <u>Come off it!</u> He's more
interested in mixing with the glamour pusses and upper echelon
high-fliers that are worming their way into her good books. So
my kid brother's gay. What's new. Who isn't. *TELL THAT TO THE MARINES!*
Sure I know what you'll say when you read this Mum. You'll say I'm
ungrateful. <u>I know that scenario. I've done that trip. Been there.
Done that.</u> Just because you keep swamping my bank account with
money. What kind of substitute is that? Thanks for the world trips
Mum. <u>Thanks for nothing!</u>
Iguess you have given me one thing Edna Dearest - ANOREXIA NERVOS
Gift wrapped. THANKS A BUNDLE. All my dollies and sweeties were
always
~~always~~ locked up or given to Kenny. No wonder my hormones have
gonebananas - whose wouldn't? I've had more caring compassion
from <u>store detectives</u> than you've ever given me. So I'm a between-
meal-snacker and I've been busted in more supermarkets than you've
had caviar breakfasts. Sure I'm going on twenty stone and I make
Mama Cass look like Twiggy. BIG DEAL. Your only daughter is
digging her grave with her teeth. BON APPETIT MEGASTAR. I'm the
fattest anorexic in the world. That's cool. So what's new?

Ring Lord Goodman!

THE MANUSCRIPT AT THIS STAGE BECOMES TRAGICALLY DERANGED

Me _and_ _my_ _minders_.

Sharing a joke with a _former British leader_. (left)

Guess who's checking out my accessories.

Lord and Lady Bath lionise me and I quite like them.

HORACE HEIDT

AND HIS FAMILY

HIS CREED

"Tis better to build boys
than mend men"

In Hollywood beside the tomb
of my favourite band leader
(alas not at the "Heidt" of his career).

Here's me being a fit butch in my
Brechtian Berlin bowler.

(Edna Bowles)

o great Australian Dames share a joke with my best friend. e Madge missing the point. A rare snap of my bridesmaid before landscaping

Me playing cheeky with my favourite crooner.

The young adore me though this sweet head-banger gave me the willies

A rare press shot of me reading something uncalled-for (for research purposes only

Here's me waxing winsome at the waxworks with <u>Dame Victoria</u>.

Your author trying a few <u>eyes</u> for size.

A rare shot of me relaxing with a few <u>showbiz</u> pals.

Me cuddling a kanga kiddie
Conservation conscious as
<u>always</u>.

This is Wendy my cuddly
wombat <u>in season</u>.

Here's me with two larger than life marsupials. Which is Mary Whitehouse?

Me cuddling a kiddie. Conservation conscious as always.

My son Kenneth and his sympathetic flatmate are no strangers to Dame Nature's wilder ways. They can make a fist of anything and there's nothing these two macho males can't cope with when it comes to camping around the outback.

The All Cake Diet

Old Marie Antoinette, the EEC Queen of yesteryear, is remembered today for the famous remark to her disadvantaged subjects, 'Let them eat cake.' For many years historians and Open University types thought this was a pretty ghastly, elitist thing to say to the underpriviledged, but an Australian research unit, subsidized by me incidentally, has discovered that Queen Marie was an old nutritionist and dietitian from way back. In those days EEC peasants all had weight problems due to their unhealthy diet of potatoes, swedes and turnips. Slim little Marie had discovered that cake, in all its many scrummy forms, can, when eaten according to a balanced regime, provide the human body with all its nutritional needs and reduce excess weight at the same time! Far from sneering at her porky peasants, their modern-minded Monarch was proffering them the patisserie passport out of Cellulite City.

The average slice of cake contains most of the things our organism craves. Roughage for the bowel; glucose to give us essential energy; fruit or fruit solids to keep our systems regular; not to mention soluble solids of cake, edible cake fats, edible colouring and precious lecithin solids, niacin, riboflavin, tripoxaline, lanolin, tincture of cubeb, squibb, homogenized mineral compounds, UHT, vitamin derivatives and trace elements.

The reason that cake consumption has for so many years been linked with obesity is entirely due to foolish people mixing cake with other fattening foodstuffs like steak, chips, eggs, fruit and salads. If you give the All Cake Diet a trial of only one week you will be amazed how you feel at the end of it.

DAY 1

Breakfast No more than 3 chocolate éclairs or $1\frac{1}{2}$ Florentines.
Lunch Treat yourself to a $\frac{1}{4}$ lb slice of frozen blackcurrant cheesecake, and if you are still hungry you are allowed one macaroon.
Supper Your first exciting All Cake Supper will prove surprisingly satisfying, and believe it or not you are allowed one large strawberry flan and 6 brandy snaps. Mmmmmmmmm! Slimming can be scrummy!

DAY 2

Breakfast Sorry, still just 3 chocolate éclairs to start your day, but if you get peckish mid-morning a nice thick slice of Dundee fruit cake will fill the gap.
Lunch A light lunch of lemon meringue pie will send you satisfied through the afternoon.
Dinner Dine on 6 rhum babas. And for dessert – how does a plateful of profiteroles sound?

DAY 3

As you face your early morning éclair breakfast you will start to feel your wonderful new All Cake Diet beginning to 'bite'. Watch the others putting on pounds of yukky fat with their eggs and bacon as you nibble your way through your bonus Lamington (an Australian cake dipped in luscious coconut). Lunch today is a figure-trimming Victoria sponge garnished with kiwi fruit, and for supper try an hors d'œuvre of vanilla slice followed by a juicy $\frac{1}{2}$ lb segment of mocha gateau or Madeira cake.

DAY 4

After your usual breakfast, lunch on a pineapple and passion fruit pavlova, New Zealand's world-famous meringue cake, as much as you can eat. And for dinner this evening you have earned as much trifle as you can swallow, with lashings of cream and sherry. Who said a diet was no fun?

DAY 5

There are 6 chocolate éclairs on the menu this morning, and what do you say to a lunch of apple strudel and pineapple upside-down cake? Sorry, no more than 2 lb (0.907 kilos). For supper that classic Austrian speciality, hazelnut and raspberry meringue cake made with 5 eggs and 10 fl oz of whipping cream.

DAY 6

Breakfast as usual with 3 supplementary Lamingtons. Lunch on coconut cream cake with strawberry fondue frosting, and for dinner something rich and fruity – 2 lb of carrot and banana cake.

DAY 7

Bravo! You are unlikely by now to want to go back to your wicked old ways. In fact many people I know who have got as far as this with the All Cake Diet have found the smell of conventional foods makes them physically sick. That's O.K. too, Possums – being sick is Dame Nature's oldest slimming secret. Day 7 is a bit tough because we're only allowed an old-fashioned English treacle tart for lunch, but for dinner an entire Black Forest gateau is yours down to the last yummy mouthful, and look at me, Possums. I'm slimmmmmmmmm!

WORLD COPYRIGHT: *The All Cake Diet*, Dame Edna Everage

Popular Bedstains and

ALCOHOL

Add glycerine to washing water, rinse sheets with vinegar (or use household bleach, but only with fast cottons); wash in detergent, rinse in hydrogen peroxide.

BEER

Sponge with water to which *a little* ammonia has been added, or rinse in warm vinegar water. Failing this, apply a weak hydrogen peroxide solution to the sheet or mattress and leave to dry in the sun. Wash in 'usual' way. If bedding is not washable, soak stain with methylated spirit and work in a little soap with the fingers. Let dry, brush out.

BLOOD (!)

If wet, soak in cold water first, then add a few drops of household ammonia to the water. If dry blood, soak in a solution of one dessertspoon of salt to three cups of water. Bleach is good for fast cottons. On non-washing material cover with a cold paste of laundry starch and brush off when dry. Repeat until stain disappears. If no starch, use cornflour.

CHEWING GUM

Rub sheets over with an icecube from the refrigerator, then rub with eucalyptus, or kerosene, or put sheet in plastic bag in refrigerator for several hours, then it will peel off. Remove from skin with butter or polyunsaturated equivalent. If it is in the hair rub some peanut butter into it, then wipe off with a tissue.
WATCHPOINT: THIS APPLIES ONLY TO SCALP HAIR

CHOCOLATE

First soak fabric in cold water containing detergent. Don't use hot water, it sets the stain. For fast cottons (if stain is still there) use bleach; for woollens, borax. Also try rubbing the spot with glycerine and leaving on for ten minutes before washing. If choc stain is fresh try sucking with clean gums

COCOA

Hold bedclothes over basin and pour boiling water through. If stain has dried, rub in some powdered borax or detergent and leave for a few hours. Wash or suck in the usual way.

How to Banish Them

GREASE

Sponge with eucalyptus or cleaning fluid after blotting with blotting paper. Nail polish remover is also good but do not use it on artificial silk.

HAIR OIL
(ALSO EFFICACIOUS WITH NIVEA))

Make a paste of french (or EEC) chalk and dry-cleaning fluid and spread on marks fairly thickly. Let dry, brush off.

LIPSTICK

Sponge with cold water and rub glycerine or eucalyptus into the mark with fingertips before washing. Non-washable fabrics should be sponged with grease solvent. Sometimes eau-de-cologne shifts it too (something Ken came up with).

MEDICINE
(ON SENIOR'S SLUMBERWEAR)

Sponge with lukewarm water and clean with white, unstarched cloths, changing cloths as often as possible, working from the outer edge towards the centre.

MILDEW

Remove by rubbing well into spot equal quantities of salt, starch and soft soap. At night soak in milk. Next day wash in detergent. Repeat if necessary. If still not out put paste on both sides and put in sun to dry.

PEN MARKS

Remove with toothpaste on a soft cloth.

TEA

Treat immediately by pouring boiling water through from a height. Rub with lemon juice and hang in the sun. Repeat if necessary

URINE ETC.

Sponge with mild ammonia solution or bicarbonate of soda solution to neutralize, or sponge with *warm* salt water or lemon juice or white wine vinegar. Wash as usual and rinse in ammonia water.

CHUNDER

Remove yukkiness with dry cloths. Wash with bicarbonate of soda in warm water, then with detergent solution. Dry with clean dry cloths.

KEYS

DAME EDNA'S LEVÉE

(Featured on pages 120–21), photographed in the Oliver Messel Suite, The Dorchester. From left to right:

1 Russell my chauffeur
2 Felicity my personal florist and glad-sexer
3 Dot my manicurist
4 Samson my North London coiffeur
5 Kevin my overworked postie
6 Lord Timbers, Photographer by Appointment
7 Gideon Bible deliverer
8 Sidonie and Abigail, two of Madge's circle I'm afraid
9 Cathy my colonic irrigator
10 Nancy my senior secretary
11 Daniel my chef
12 Ken Thomson my PRO and archivist
13 Andy my wombat handler
14 Dr Othmar Schoek my Swiss adviser
15 Irmgard my minder
16 'Mr Cartier' with my trinket tray
17 Wendy the wombat
(Absent from this study for some reason best known to themselves are Barry Humphries my manager, Lord Everage my husband, and Mrs Douglas Allsop my companion.)

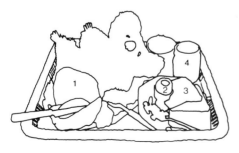

POOLSIDE PLATTER

(Featured on page 117), photographed at The Sanctuary at the Dance Centre, London. From

1 Parma Koala
2 Platypus du Jour
3 Nivea Toast
4 Marmite de Vegemite

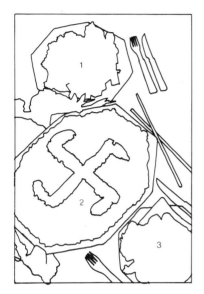

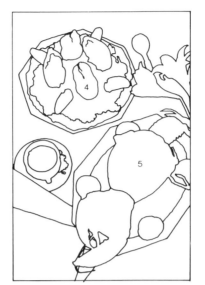

(Featured on pages 122-4; most of the recipes can be discovered on pages 125-9.) From left

1 Lizard Island Omelette de Pineapple à la John Gordon
2 Savoury Australian Chillied Sausages à la Bert Brecht
3 Green Fire – for the Jaded Palate
4 Pork 'n Zola
5 Lobster stuffed Marrow with Campari sauce

Solution to crossword featured on page 98.

6 Honolulu Black Puddings
7 Hot Banana and Sweetcorn Smoothie (for recipe see page 18)
8 Honolulu Black Puddings served with Peppermint Chocolate Chip Ice Cream

Many people often ask me about my Family Shield and so here, for the first historic time, I publish my Armorial Bearings. Of course, as a woman, my Arms must be linked to those of my male spouse and hence the left-hand (or Dexter) side of the Shield, commemorating Norm's work for the Victorian Water Board. The other little elements need no introduction.

For those who are curious about the colouring of the artwork (since Lord Nicolson could not run to colour on this page) I publish the following, prepared by my favourite and devoted Heralds:

TINCTURING TIPS

Arms: Dexter Azure Guttée d'Argent a Tap Or (Everage) *impaling* Argent between in chief and base a representation of the Sydney Opera House and in fess a Funnel-web Spider and an Australian Blow-fly Proper Two Stems of Gladioli in saltire Or (Beasley) Supporters: To the Dexter an Australian Shark Proper attired in Australian Eye-wear Carnation And to the Sinister a Ring-tailed Possum guardant Proper likewise attired Bleu Celeste.

Watchpoint: Provided my Shield and Supporters are tinctured authentically, Readers may adopt their preferred metal, colour or fur for my Order Ribbon and Scroll.

166

BY APPOINTMENT TO DAME EDNA EVERAGE

Ken Thomson, Public Relations Officer, Archivist and Editor Emeritus

Jane Frazer, Personal Assistant

Julian Jebb, Spiritual Adviser by Appointment

Carl Davis, Master of the Dame's Music

John Timbers, Photographer by Appointment

Charlie Waite, Photographer by Appointment

Susan Greenhill, Photographer by Appointment

Victor Arwas, Curator and Art Adviser by Appointment

Charles Osborne, Literary Adviser by Appointment

Ian Tasker, Production Superviser by Appointment

Jane Hamilton, Mistress of the Dame's Wardrobe

Billy Goodwin, Master of the Dame's Wardrobe

Helen Salter, Adviser on Folklore and Domestic Hygiene by Appointment

Dr Adrienne Clark, Horticulturist by Appointment

Dr Ida Lichter, Recorder of the Dame's REMS

Frank Gardiner, Maker of the Dame's Nightie

John Gordon, Pineapple Dance Centre, Maître de Danse

Henry Gray, M.V.O., Artist by Appointment

Patric Dickinson, Rouge Dragon Pursuivant of Arms

Terence McCarthy, Executive Herald by Appointment

Judy Walker, Penny Harvey, Penny Hatchick, Buyers by Appointment

Annie Morris, Sue Graham, Jay Whitcombe, Photographers' Assistants

Les Sharp, Builder by Appointment

Norman, Dave and Charlie of Tielynn Motors Ltd, Bed-welding Consultants

Patrick Boyce, A Sleeping Companion

Derek Davies, A Sleeping Companion

Mario Chang, A Sleeping Companion

Ignazio Moneta, Chauffeur

Lisa Kaye, A Bathing Companion

Richard Bonte, A Model

David Todd, Photographer by Appointment

Robert Lamb, Entomologist in Residence

Mark Simmonds, Kim Knott, Paul Oakley, David Young, Provincial Artistic Advisers by Appointment

Jan Wood, Knitter in Residence

Tan Siew Kheng, Air Hostess by Appointment

Neil Burton, Architectural Consultant

Jill Hollis, Personal Librarian

The Dorchester, an Hotel, Park Lane, London

Super Body, Beauty and Health Club by Appointment

The Sanctuary at the Dance Centre, Beauty and Health Club by Appointment

Singapore Airlines, by Appointment

Maples, Purveyors of Furniture by Appointment

Stokecroft Arts, Ltd, Purveyors of Beds by Appointment

Editions Graphiques Ltd, Purveyors of Art by Appointment

Arding and Hobbs, Clapham Junction, London, The Complete Departmental Store by Appointment

Cartier Ltd, Purveyor of Jewellery by Appointment

Gwyneth Salusbury Associates, Publicity Consultants by Appointment

London Bedding Centre, Knightsbridge, Supplier of Bedding by Appointment (turquoise valance in polyester/cotton)

Peter Reed, Supplier of Bedding by Appointment (lemon sheets in 100% cotton with two-row cord, rose pillowcases in 100% cotton percale with embroidered scalloped border)

Marks and Spencer p.l.c., Supplier of Bedding by Appointment (St Michael bedspread in 50% polyester/cotton)

David Mellor, Purveyor of Kitchen Equipment by Appointment

The Telephone Box, Supplier of Telephones by Appointment

The Pan Bookshop, Purveyor of Books by Appointment

The Australian Gift Shop, Purveyor of Gifts by Appointment

Sidney Smith (Chelsea) Ltd, A Boutique

Gerard (Hire) Ltd, Wombat Supplier by Appointment

Sata-Lite Gift Centre, Supplier of Lamps by Appointment

Manor Aquatics, Supplier of Wombat Leads by Appointment

Laffeaty's Ltd, Supplier of Teddy Bears by Appointment

International Car Hire Ltd, Supplier of Limousines by Appointment

Lord Weidenfeld of Chelsea, Publisher by Appointment
Russell Ash and Felicity Luard, Editors in Domo
Andrew Kay, Art Director and Senior Design Consultant
Daniel Rainey, Illustrator by Appointment
Julia Brown and Cathy Ellis, Picture Researchers by Appointment
Joy FitzSimmons, Art Assistant by Appointment

PHOTOGRAPHIC ACKNOWLEDGEMENTS

John Timbers: frontispiece, 18, 22, 29–34, 36, 54–5, 63–5, 75, 78–9, 83
(top), 101, 118–24, 129

Charlie Waite: 11, 23, 35, 43, 47, 52, 57, 58–60, 66–7, 77, 111–15, 116, 117,
137–8, 158–61

Susan Greenhill: 50, 72–4, 76, 81 (bottom), 134–5, 153 (top); 17, 90, 154 (bottom) Australian
News and Information Bureau, London; 20 Libertine Magazine; 42 (from left to right) Turin
Royal Library, Les Films la Boetie; Archiv fur Kunst und Geschichte, Berlin, Beth
Hatefutsoth, The Nahum Goldmann Museum of the Jewish Diaspora, The Imperial War
Museum, London, The Mansell Collection, London; 69, 71, 89, 131 (top) Mary Evans Picture
Library, London; 70 Nationalmuseet, Copenhagen; 83 (bottom) Photo: David Todd; 88
Photo: Ronald Chapman; 90 (4) Allsport Photographic. Photo: Tony Duffy; 130 Alte
Pinakothek, Munich; 131 (bottom) National Gallery, London; 132–3 The Louvre Collection,
Paris; 149 (top), 151 Mirror Group Newspapers; 150 (top), Boloks Photography. Photo: Judi
Lesta, (bottom) BBC; 152 (top), 155 (bottom) Photo: Vicki Hansen; 152 (bottom) Gay
News. Photo: Bob Workman; 154 (top) Photo: Geoff McKell; 155 (top) Melbourne Sun.

Endpapers by Class 4, Greencroft Primary School, Clifton, Nottingham

DAME EDNA IS A DIVISION OF THE BARRY HUMPHRIES GROUP.